Health, healing and wholeness

Centre for
Faith and Spirituality
Loughborough University
HOWARD BOOTH

kevin
mayhew

First published in 1998 by
Arthur James Ltd

Published in 2002 by
KEVIN MAYHEW LTD
Buxhall, Stowmarket, Suffolk, IP14 3BW
Email: info@kevinmayhewltd.com

9 8 7 6 5 4 3 2 1 0

ISBN 1 84003 925 6
Catalogue Number 1500517

Front cover design by Angela Selfe
Typesetting by Richard Weaver
Printed and bound in Great Britain

Contents

A Note to Readers

Different typefaces are used in this book to indicate the sections:

The main text is set in this Garamond type. Within each main chapter are discussion questions indicated by a fist, thus ☞, and each chapter ends with a set of specific questions in italic, which summarise the chapter and which are intended for deep personal thought or for discussion in groups.

There then follows a separate section headed 'Words for Thought, Prayer and Meditation', which is set in Abadi typeface like this.

Acknowledgements

Some of the material in Chapters 5 and 6 has already been included in articles published in *The Health and Healing Bulletin* of the Methodist Church and in *The Epworth Review*. However, both chapters have been worked on and considerably revised.

I was greatly helped in preparing Chapter 3 on Prayer and Healing by a stimulating sabbatical study by the Revd David Boyle and appreciate most warmly his co-operation.

I have used a number of short quotations from various authors throughout the book and especially in the devotional chapters. The source of the quotations has been given in the text itself but I now set out in alphabetical order the titles, authors and publishers of all the books or articles that I have been able to trace. A few of the quotations I have copied down in my commonplace book from addresses which I have heard or from books and magazines I have seen in libraries and have had on loan. I have not always been able to supply the full details of these. I gratefully acknowledge my indebtedness to all these writers, both living and dead. If there has been any infringement of copyright or inadequate acknowledgement I sincerely apologise and will make amendments in any future editions.

Adam, David, *The Cry of the Deer,* Triangle.
Barth, Karl, *Dogmatics in Outline,* SCM Press.
Bell, John and Maule, Graham, *Eh Jesus, Yes Peter,* Wild Goose Publications.
Boulding, Maria, *The Coming of God,* Fount Paperbacks.
Cooke, Bernard, *Christian Involvement,* Argus Communications.
Dale, Alan, *New World,* Oxford University Press.
Gardner, Rex, *Healing Miracles,* Darton, Longman and Todd.
Gunstone, John, *The Lord Is Our Healer,* Hodder and Stoughton.
Hammarskjöld, Dag, *Markings,* Alfred A. Knopf.

Hick, John, *Evil and the God of Love,* Harper and Row.
Jefferies, Esmond, *The Power and the Glory,* Arthur James.
le Shan, Robert, *Holistic Living,* Turnstone Press.
Long, Anne, *Listening,* Daybreak.
Moltmann, Jurgen, *The Power and the Powerless,* SCM Press.
Motyer, J., *The Message of James,* Inter-Varsity Fellowship.
Perry, Michael (ed.), *Deliverance,* SPCK.
Pherigo, Lindsay P., *The Great Physician,* Abingdon Press.
Pietroni, Patrick, *Holistic Living,* Dent Paperbacks.
Richards, John, *Faith and Healing,* John Richards.
Brother Roger of Taizé, *Parable of Community,* Mowbrays.
Smaile, Tom, *CCHH Annual Lecture 1992,* CCHH.
Taylor, Allegra, *I Fly Out With Bright Feathers,* Fontana Collins.
Taylor, Harold, *Sent To Heal,* The Order of St Luke (Australia).
Vanstone, W. H., *Fare Well in Christ,* Darton, Longman and Todd.
Ward, Neville, *The Use of Praying,* Epworth Press.
Ward Jones, A., *Psychological Perspectives in Ministry* (an article on relationships between general practitioners and clergy), Gracewing.
Wilkinson, John, *Health and Healing,* Handsel Press.
Wimber, John, *Power Healing,* Hodder and Stoughton.
Wright, Frank, *The Pastoral Nature of Healing,* SCM Press.
Various authors in *The Christian Parapsychologist,* magazine articles.

The following books are my own writings which have been briefly referred to in the text:

Healing Experiences, The Bible Reading Fellowship (op).
Healing Is Wholeness, The Methodist Church and the CCHH (op).
Healing Through Caring, Arthur James (op).
In Search of Health and Wholeness (ed.), The Methodist Church (op).
Prayer Tools for Health and Healing, The Grail.
Seven Whole Days – A Health and Healing Worship Book, Arthur James (op).

The brief extracts from the writings of Julian of Norwich, Mechtilde of Magdeburg, William Temple, Elizabeth Cheney, Rosalind Rinker, St John of the Cross, Thomas Merton, Henri Nouwen, Helen Keller, Archbishop Ramsey, Ian M. Fraser, George Herbert, Baldwin of Ford, Ladislas M. Orsy, and the poem 'The Creed of Liberty' by Phoebe Willets are taken from my commonplace book so I have no trace of their origins. The words from Chester Cathedral can be found written on its famous clock. The poem by William Wordsworth, 'Lines above Tintern Abbey', is included in a wide variety of poetry anthologies. Bible quotations are from the Revised English Bible.

About the author

HOWARD BOOTH came into the Church's healing ministry in the early 1960s because he himself needed to find an inner healing. Eventually he became Chairman of the Methodist Church's Pastoral and Healing Committee, and then for the last five years of his active ministry served nationally within that Church as its Health and Healing Advisor. Throughout these years he has conducted hundreds of conferences, quiet days, seminars and retreats, and still continues to do so. He has written six previous books and numerous pamphlets, booklets and articles. Now retired and over 70, he loves to walk the Derbyshire dales with his wife, Alice, and plays indoor tennis with her and other seniors at the local Leisure Centre.

Credo

I believe . . .

1. that Jesus healed and cured people as it is recorded in the New Testament but that the healing he offered was of the whole person and included repentance and forgiveness;

2. that there can be healing without cure as happened in the case of St Paul and his 'thorn in the flesh';

3. that there can be cure without healing as is often the case when the emphasis is upon the removal of symptoms rather than upon the wholeness of the person;

4. that God does not will experiences of pain and suffering but that he can use these experiences when they happen to bring needy people closer to him and also to enable observers of the human condition to think hard about life's meaning;

5. that health in the fullest sense of body, mind and spirit is something to be cherished and that proper diet, physical exercise, inward release through confession and sharing are all part of the health-maintaining process;

6. that different people come into the world with different health potential due to the inheritance they receive from genetic factors, proper bonding and the warmth of sincere parental love;

7. that some people do have a healing gift which can be developed by medical and pastoral training and that this gift is always enhanced when it is offered in dedication to Jesus Christ;

8. that ordinary Christians can help needy people by being channels of grace and peace. This happens through prayerful concern and genuine love. The art of listening is part of this and even naturally good listeners can become more able through simple training;

9. in modern medicine and the development of scientific technology, but that when the fruits of these are combined with the establishment of caring relationships there is always a deeper outcome;

10. that the healing acts of Jesus were demonstrations of his Lordship, and that they have the secondary purpose of making us think deeply about the ways in which we relate to other people.

HOWARD BOOTH
October 1997

Introduction

In Search of Health and Wholeness was the title of a book published by the Methodist Church's Division of Social Responsibility in 1985. I was the editor of this book, which sold over 6,000 copies and was widely used both within and beyond the Methodist Church. Since then many books on the subject of health and healing have appeared and there has been much water under the bridge. I have been responsible for five of these myself: *Healing Is Wholeness* (CCHH and DSR); *Healing Experiences* (BRF); *Healing Through Caring* (Arthur James); *Prayer Tools for Health and Healing* (The Grail); and *Seven Whole Days – A Health and Healing Worship Book* (Arthur James).

A number of the books which have appeared have been anecdotal. They have their place and it is always encouraging to hear about positive real life situations although care must always be exercised to make sure that enthusiasm does not embellish the facts. The experience of those who are involved in what is now called the Christian Healing Ministry seems to differ widely. Some like the Revd Tom Smaile speak only of a few healing happenings of an unusual nature. A survey by the Revd Michael T. Fermer about the healing ministry in Anglican Churches indicated that he had not observed many healings which could be considered as miraculous. He strongly affirmed the wider meaning of the word healing, through counselling, pastoral care, love, patient listening and fellowship, growth in understanding, changes in society and medical care. Others, like Esmond Jefferies in his book *The Power and the Glory* (Arthur James), tell of numerous healing incidents. John Gunstone (who I have heard described as an enlightened charismatic) also has fascinating stories to tell, although in a calm and restrained manner. See his book *The Lord Is Our Healer* (Hodder) and others.

Within the Christian healing ministry itself there is a variety of emphases. One of the authors mentioned above (Esmond Jefferies) encourages those he is trying to help to relax under a mild form of hypnotism. Then he encourages *visualisation,* inviting his clients to see Jesus in their situations and laying his hands upon them. He is ready and willing to see individual people many times and although he is the pioneer of a healing fellowship he does not practise his healing ministry in the presence of large crowds. Others, like the well known Dr Morris Cerillo, seem to function only with large crowds who are encouraged to see and feel things happening to them instantaneously. Of all the present-day mass healing movements in Great Britain, his has come in for the strongest criticism, not least in programmes on television presented by the BBC.

Others emphasise *the casting out of demons.* This is certainly a feature of the work initiated by Philip Horrabin, and now centred in **Ellel Grange**, near Lancaster, and also I gather in a new **Ellel** in the south of England. Some of those most active are suspicious of others whose theological basis and pastoral practice is different. My observation, based on the practical experience of views expressed at my own meetings and conferences, is that those within charismatic renewal circles who emphasise the casting out of demons do not approve of the use of hypnotism, which they regard as being demonic in itself.

Then again the healing movements in the main line churches originated in different ways. Within my own Church, the Methodist Church, it was the late Dr Leslie Weatherhead who emphasised healing which came about from *deeper self-understanding using the insights of psychotherapy.* He also used mild hypnosis in treating his clients and it was Dr Weatherhead's work which inspired Esmond Jefferies. There was also a significant emphasis on prayer for individual people and almost always on Sunday evenings the massive City Temple congregation would be invited to spend time in prayer for one particular needy person. Out of Dr Weatherhead's pioneer work came the *counselling input* under the leadership and inspiration of the late Dr William (Bill) Kyle, founder of the **Westminster Pastoral Foundation**. It is significant that one of the earliest organised healing movements within the Methodist Church was the **Methodist Society for Medical and Pastoral Psychology**.

In a related way the **Clinical Theology** movement, inspired by the late Dr Frank Lake, emphasised the counselling relationship but added another dimension, that of helping his patients to become aware of what happened to them prior to birth. If the expectant mother with a child in the womb experienced severe stress and anxiety then those negative feelings would be transmitted to the unborn child. This could be further complicated by a traumatic birth. Dr Lake's treatments sought to take needy people back into those pre-birth experiences, at first using a now-banned drug LSD-25. The importance of *birth scripts* becoming *life scripts* has been taken up by two Irish Catholic women, Shirley Ward and Alison Hunter, who operate from **The Amethyst Centre**, near to Dublin. They believe that we are able to transfer our own healing energies by the *laying on of hands.* Shirley Ward is described as a *Pre- and Peri-natal Psychotherapist.*

Yet another strand can be discerned in the work and witness of the **Guild of St Raphael**, an Anglican organisation, which centres in a deeply sacramental theology in which the Eucharist is the main way in which we meet Christ the Healer. Then there is the *Order of St Luke the Physician* which was founded in the USA in 1947. It is evangelical in its basis but has a broad outlook embracing several different emphases within contemporary evangelicalism. Another organisation with a distinguished history is the **Guild of Health**. The emphasis here is upon relaxation, prayer and meditation. **The Acorn Christian Healing Trust** was founded by Bishop Maddocks and his wife Anne, originally to provide him with support for his work as the Advisor on Healing to the Archbishops of Canterbury and York. It has now developed into one of the major organisations promoting the healing ministry, not only in the Church of England but right across the denominational boundaries. It has a considerable full-time and part-time staff with impressive headquarters at Whitehill Chase, High Street, Bordon, Hampshire, GU35 0AP. The Acorn Trust embraces a variety of approaches to Christian healing. One of its main features has been the bringing together of *Apostolic Pairs,* one of whom has medical training. They give a focus for the healing movement in their areas. The establishment of training courses in *Christian Listening* under the overall direction of the Revd Anne Long, has been another contribution which Acorn has made to the whole Church. Bishop Maddocks recently retired and his successor is the Revd Russ Parker, also an Anglican priest but with an earlier background in the Pentecostal Church.

Most of the groups mentioned above were brought together under the umbrella of the **Churches' Council for Health and Healing** which had been started in 1944 inspired by the concerns of Archbishop William Temple. As early as 1924, when Bishop of Manchester, he had told his diocesan conference: 'You cannot read the gospels and cut out the ministry of healing without tearing them to ribbons . . . [Nor can you] draw a sharp line between what is physical and what is mental. The two merge into each other in most baffling ways.' I was Vice-Chairman of CCHH for five years during the '80s and all involved became aware that the various denominational churches and other bodies involved were failing to give adequate financial support for an effective organisation. In spite of this much good work was done especially when the Revd Dr Denis Duncan was its part-time Director. I recall some memorable national conferences at Swanwick with over 300 people present. At the last one of these the keynote speaker was Archbishop Robert Runcie. However in 1999 when Bishop John Perry was Chairman an enquiry was conducted which led to a decision to close CCHH down.

Whilst this was happening the Church of England through the House of Bishops had established a working party 'to assess the theological understanding and the state of the Ministry of Healing in the Church of England and to make recommendations as to its improved effectiveness, taking into account not only the activities of different groups but also the ecumenical expression of this ministry'. The Chairman of this working party was none other than Bishop John Perry (Bishop of Chelmsford) who, as noted above, was the last Chairman of CCHH before its demise. One of the recommendations of the working party contained in an effective and substantial report entitled *A Time to Heal* (published in 2000 by Church House Publishing) was that 'a new Churches' Healing Ministry Group (CHMG) should be set up for the ecumenical co-ordination, support and promotion of the healing ministry of Jesus Christ'. So it would appear that CCHH was needed but that a new start should be made with a new title. In my judgement this, whilst at first seeming rather ironical, was a wise recommendation. CCHH carried with it a great deal of baggage from the past. The new group could make a fresh start.

What has happened is that the Joint Methodist/United Reformed Churches Development Group with Baptist and Anglican observers took the initiative to liaise with the Revd Bill Snelson of Churches Together in England (CTE) with the hope of establishing a new ecumenical forum to be known as Churches Together for Healing (presumably CTH). This is in its early stages but a promising start has been made and enquiries can be directed to Revd Bill Snelson, CTE, 27 Tavistock Square, London, WC1 9HH. A website is being prepared to disseminate information.

One vital area which must be given priority for these new developments is that of co-operation between the Church, its clergy and ministers and the medical profession. This was one of Archbishop William Temple's main concerns and for a time this was fulfilled by **The Institute of Religion and Medicine (IRM)**. This was a separate group originally with individual membership and some field study groups. It had however become subsumed within the Churches' Council for Health and Healing and become known as **CCHH Medical Forum**. This has now been lost with the demise of CCHH and must be revived in one form or another.

The above is a brief history of some of the main developments that have taken place in the Christian Healing Ministry in the last half-century. Why now another book which may seem to cover already familiar territory?

Many of the splendid books which are available do not lend themselves easily to being the basis for study groups in the ever-increasing number of Churches who want to understand more about the healing ministry and then want to develop its practice in simple but significant ways. There are also numbers of individuals who wish to pursue a course of study from their home bases. These include many ministers who want to make the subject the basis of a sabbatical study. I have led and participated in literally hundreds of conferences, seminars and retreats over the past 30 years and I have been made aware of the need for some simple, basic material which does not seek to persuade those who use it to one particular point of view or approach. I have often said that I have learned more from those with whom I disagree than from those who see things in the same way as I do. Thus at certain points in the study chapters I have set out differing views in what I believe is a fair and reasonable manner. I have also provided issues to stimulate thought within each of the chapters and then questions at the end either as the basis of group discussion or for individuals to provide written answers. I have also sought to help those using the book to move to considered judgements which call for action. In many instances my own convictions have been clearly revealed but I do not think that I am always right and I have moved my own position from time to time in the light of reflection and prayer.

This brings me to the 'Words for Thought, Prayer and Meditation' which follow each study chapter. These are intended to provide a framework for a devotional exercise in which the fruits of study can be offered to God and clearer understanding sought from God himself through the guidance of the Holy Spirit. Many good things can flow from study and the sharing of ideas but many more good things can come from them being grounded in prayer and quiet, reflective meditation. This conviction has led me in recent years to concentrate more on quiet days than on conferences! To enable healing experiences has been my aim and to promote deep inner healing which all of us need more than anything else. Those who are discovering a greater wholeness have more resources with which to face the challenge of illness when it comes – and then to face the ultimate challenge of death.

In the introduction to his book *Power Healing*, the late John Wimber writes:

> As you read these pages I urge you not to seek formulas for gaining a temporary reprieve from death; I urge you to seek the Lord and Lifegiver himself, Jesus Christ. That way, regardless of the visible results, your prayers will always have power for healing.

I do not always agree with everything John Wimber says, but I would wholeheartedly endorse these words.

1
The Health and Healing Scene: An Arena of God's Activity

Things are happening right across the board in the field of health and healing. The more obvious developments in the world of scientific medicine we hear a great deal about. New drugs and improved surgical techniques just happen year after year. Many of them are simple refinements and improvements upon existing practices – but they all matter and they all make a difference. There are, however, other significant developments both within modern medicine and also on its fringes. The first one to consider is . . .

The growth of concern for the medicine of the person

The 'medicine of the person' was a phrase first coined by the late Paul Tournier and it was an idea he explored in his many books. It was meant to supplement and extend the so-called 'medical model' concept. This sought to identify a particular problem and isolate it prior to treatment with drugs, surgery or perhaps an altered lifestyle. This model and its application has proved to be tremendously successful and we all owe a great deal to it. However, one negative consequence is that there has developed in popular culture the idea that one day, in the not far distant future, there will be a pill or a procedure for every ill. Every possible form of illness will be thus dealt with and we shall all live to a ripe old age and then just fall away into the experience of dying.

Paul Tournier and many who have followed him see things differently. Their emphasis is described as holistic and they speak of not treating the illness but treating the person. It is accepted that the causes of illness are often complicated and far reaching. If there is division and conflict within the total being of the person concerned, the origins of the illness may lie in that breakdown of harmony. It is in this area that the influences of mind and spirit upon bodily functions come into play. One physician described a man's peptic ulcer as being caused by his having an over-ambitious wife! The inference being that the pressure put upon him by his wife always wanting to move up the social scale was such that his stomach wall developed an ulcer. This could be dealt with by modern scientific medicine but this was not the ultimate answer. Some new form of accommodation and understanding with his wife could have more lasting therapeutic consequences.

When Dr Peter Nixon, an eminent cardiologist, addressed the annual meeting of the Churches' Council for Health and Healing some years ago, he told us of how he suggested to some of his patients that they go away for a time of retreat, relaxation and reassessment. This could make all the difference to their future health and well-being. An adjusted lifestyle was just as necessary as any drugs or surgery, although sometimes both were needed.

The influence of the environment upon the origins and development of certain forms of illness is an additional factor. During the miners' strike in the '70s doctors' surgeries were crowded with patients seeking pain relievers, anti-depressants, etc. The miners and their families were medicalising their social problems.

A similar situation occurred in the town of Calne in Wiltshire for so long the base for the manufacture of Harris meat products – sausages, pies, etc. A decision was taken to move the whole operation away from Calne over a period of years. A young GP with a practice in the town took the opportunity to study the effects of this move upon the health of the patients on his list. The results were so striking as to encourage him to write an article for a medical journal. The insecurity caused by this move caused all kinds of illness symptoms to develop.

Dr Patrick Pietroni founded the British Holistic Medical Association and has described his approach in a book entitled *Holistic Living* (Dent Paperbacks). One of his practices when seeing a new patient is to draw a circle which he states represents the upper surface of a cake. He then inserts a shaded slice which he uses to indicate the symptoms being presented by the patient. He goes on to tell them that whilst he will pay close attention to the symptoms they indicate, he will also be looking carefully at 'the rest of the cake'; in other words the whole person, as the real problem may lie in some other part of the body or in some kind of interpersonal conflict. If this is so then to clear up the symptom may just be to put a patch over what may well be a more fundamental problem. It is this deeper issue which needs to be discovered and exposed and, in all probability, renewed health lies in greater self-awareness and a more positive tackling of personal and sometimes social problems.

☞ *Are you aware of any of these developments affecting the GP practice to which you are attached? Should you try to ask how your doctor feels about such ideas? The aim should be of course to move to a more co-operative approach towards illness between doctor and patient.*

The next issue to be addressed is . . .

The growing interest and use of alternative or complementary therapies

Wherever you go today you will see clinics offering a variety of therapies to prospective patients. *Osteopathy* and *chiropractice* have long since acquired a degree of respectability. Osteopathy is the best known in the UK and its practitioners are well trained and qualified. It is usually directed towards muscular, skeletal and arthritic conditions. The treatment consists of massage, manipulation, exercise retraining and postural advice. Some osteopaths will also treat asthma and migraine. Chiropractice is very similar to osteopathy and differs only in the techniques utilised.

Acupuncture is based upon the Chinese model of health and disease. Energy flows in channels called meridians and disease occurs when the energy flow is blocked for any reason. Needles are placed in various key areas of the body and help to unblock the energy channels. The placing of the needles is an important feature and to help in this process the practitioner will listen carefully to the patient and will want to help with diet, emotional and environmental conditions. A number of medically qualified doctors have also undertaken training in acupuncture.

Herbalists, as their title suggests, use herbs for the treatment of medical conditions. Many effective drugs used in orthodox medical practice are derived from herbs, digitalis from foxgloves being the best-known example. Herbalists are trained in basic anatomy, physiology and diagnosis. Herbal treatments are generally less severe than some manufactured drugs but care needs to be exercised, especially in diagnosis.

Homeopathy has a long and well accepted history in the UK having been favoured by members of the royal family and having its own hospitals in some great centres like Liverpool. Homeopaths are usually trained and qualified doctors who have decided to add homeopathic treatments to the range of therapies which they offer. They describe the substances which they use as *remedies* rather than drugs. These remedies are minute doses of substances which if taken in much larger doses would produce the symptoms the patient is describing. The fundamental principle of homeopathy is that 'like cures like'. The difference between homeopathic medicines and modern drugs is that whereas modern drugs suppress or destroy a symptom or infection, homeopathic treatments stimulate the body's self-healing powers. This is achieved through the 'like cures like' principle. Homeopathy is a safe form of treatment and helps many people with less severe, non-life-threatening forms of illness. There is little evidence of its value in more serious conditions. Care should be exercised in consulting lay homeopaths, i.e. those who are not also medically qualified.

There are many other alternative or complementary therapies, some of which are variations on the methods described above. *Reflexology* for instance utilises the pressure points on the feet to stimulate the same kind of energy release as we have described in acupuncture. *Aromatherapy* utilises scented oils in massage and is a most soothing and relaxing process.

When the BMA set up a working party to study alternative or complementary therapies one of the conclusions they reached was that such therapists had certain qualities to offer which was not always the case with the more orthodox medical practitioners. These were *time, touch and compassion.* The value of these three factors in the therapeutic relationship is very high indeed. My own feeling is that the nature of the person of the practitioner is an important factor in what happens as the result of all alternative or complementary therapies.

But this is also true of orthodox medical practitioners and indeed of all the members of the helping and caring professions.

In any study course examining the above issues on the basis of a Christian commitment and Christian concerns for health and healing issues, the question is bound to be raised as to the possibility of some of the therapies we have discussed being rooted in pagan rites and non-Christian religious practices. I have not dealt with *Yoga* because I do not see it in the same category as the therapies I have described. However, it is perhaps the one discipline about which most questions are asked because of its earliest antecedents being linked with the mystery religions. Modern yoga as taught and facilitated in this country has largely left those connections behind. It is a helpful form of exercise combined with breathing techniques and relaxation practices. In other ways its benefits are similar to those offered by modern physio-therapy. Many years ago I myself was helped by reading a book entitled *Christian Yoga* written by a Baptist evangelical pastor. He had *baptised* all the yoga exercises and techniques in the name of Jesus. Anyone who has any fear about them can do the same.

The growing influence of complementary or alternative therapies is because they are gentle in their approach, give time for establishing a relationship between therapist and patient, and do not take away responsibility from the sick person. They can be a useful addition to the more generally accepted methods of orthodox medical practice. They are holistic in their understanding and generally rely upon releasing our own natural healing energies. These were described by both Schweitzer and Jung as our very own 'inner doctor'. When my generally sympathetic approach to them has been criticised in some meetings and conferences I have found it hard to understand why most of those present had not queried the particular religious faith or philosophy of their own GPs, nor that of the physicians and surgeons who have helped them whilst in hospital. Having said this I do think that some practices on the fringe of complementary therapies need to be watched very carefully. Especially is this so when things like astrology, divination, witchcraft or the use of spirit mediums appear in the overall picture. Each therapy should be examined in the light of what we believe about the centrality of Jesus. We do not want to deprive ourselves of any source of health, healing and wholeness but we do not want to compromise ourselves in any way or be a stumbling block to others. Two vital questions are: does this therapy assist me in my desire to produce the fruits of the Spirit? and, can I say of this particular practice that it enables me to acknowledge Jesus Christ as Lord?

☞ *Have you yourself any experience of an alternative or complementary therapy? Do you feel the need to be understood as a person when you are ill? Can normal medical practice from within the NHS be combined with complementary therapies? Reflect on the safeguards you would utilise and how you would discern between what is good and helpful and what may be harmful.*

Finally we must examine how there has been within all sections of the Church . . .

A rediscovery of the wholeness of the biblical doctrine of salvation

As we shall see again when we turn to study 'The Church as a Therapeutic Community' there is a close connection between the twin ideas of *being saved* in the sense of being reconciled to God through Jesus and *being made well* in the sense of being restored to health. The two verbs, *sozo* – to save, and *therapeuo* – to heal, are often used interconnectedly in the New Testament as relating to the same kind of experience. Thus salvation is an experience which we apply to the whole person. A relationship with God through Jesus brings us into a wider, more spacious world where God's spirit combines with ours to release saving/healing energies.

Various factors have been at work in the Church to promote this understanding and those factors come from varied parts of the theological spectrum. Evangelicals tended, until comparatively recently, to ignore the contemporary concern for the healing dimension, holding to the dispensational theory which was to the effect that the healing gift had been given to our Lord and to the early Church for a specific purpose, namely to endorse the acceptance of Jesus as the Messiah, the divine Son of God. This dispensation now being over, God had given us modern scientific medicine in its place. This change within the evangelical fold has largely been brought about through the influence of charismatic renewal. This both historically and now in today's Church has a strong healing emphasis. Combined with the freeing up of worship and greater openness between fellow disciples it has brought a profound sense of release and liberty which has affected all sections of the Church.

From the *sacramental wing* of the Church has come a renewed emphasis upon confession as a means of grace which opens up the healing streams of God's love. This is not always, nor indeed most often, expressed as formal confession but much more as costly sharing. This has brought about catharsis or release and has opened up a rich vein of healing.

Finally from the wing of the Church influenced by *psychological insights* has come a new understanding of the need to be loved and accepted and then to give love and extend acceptance to others. This has brought a new sense of freedom and deliverance. This was emphasised by the Revd Tom Smaile when he gave the annual lecture to the Churches' Council for Health and Healing in 1992. He was struggling to get away from the idea of an interventionist God who brought healing to some and not to others in an haphazard kind of way which caused more problems than it solved. He won over my heart and mind when he said:

> God does not over-ride and suspend natural laws, he affirms and perfects them. The natural processes are not by-passed but utilised, enhanced and made perfect by fresh contact with the creative energy of the living God from which they originally sprang.

He then went on to say:

> The restoration of the body is not as generally found as the forgiveness of sins and many who have found the latter have not necessarily found the former.

The different ways and the variety of organisations in which this movement has been held together by the ecumenical Christian Church has been outlined in the introduction to this study guide. This in itself is an indication that Christian concern for health and healing issues and the ways in which these are being tackled, both theologically and pastorally, is an idea which has always been part of Christian history but which now, in a very special way, is before us as an idea whose time has come.

☞ *Do you see God at work in all efforts being made to promote more fully human people and also a more truly human society? Does this mean that Christians can and should work happily together with those of other faiths and none? Do you accept that a person being fully human is one who has come to life in Christ?*

The way forward

Arising out of the three ways described above in which God is recognised as being at work in this important field of health and healing, the following positive statements are intended to indicate the way forward, particularly for those who name the name of Jesus and who are concerned to see proper Christian responsibility exercised in this important area of human life.

1. *It is a mistake to give undue publicity to unusual happenings. When they happen the proper course is to give quiet thanks to God who is the source of all healing. It is all too easy to get hooked on the spectacular without realising the pastoral consequences for those who seek healing as cure but do not find it.*

2. *The healing ministry is an integral part of the life of the whole Church and is expressed through its sacraments, its pastoral care and its social involvement.*

3. *The Bible has a lot to say about truly Christian attitudes towards suffering. Christian discipleship leads to involvement in the sufferings of ourselves and others; it is not a kind of insurance policy from the hurts and dilemmas of this present world.*

4. *At the same time we recognise that God's primary purpose for his children is health. To this end sickness and disease are to be fought at all levels, personal, inter-personal and social.*

5. *All those who are concerned for health, healing and wholeness should be working together. This means health care professionals, followers of*

Jesus and all who have a vision of a more fully human world in which individuals are enabled to develop their full potential.

Questions for personal written answers or to promote discussion

1. *Go through the positive statements set out above one by one. State what you believe to be absolutely central; what you believe to be of less importance and what you believe to be marginal or even questionable.*

2. *In an age when religious faith is declining some Christians seem to feel a need to have their faith reinforced by hearing about unusual and spectacular accounts of how God heals today (i.e. contemporary miracles). Books which major on such anecdotal happenings are popular and sell well. Respond to this. Does the writer of this study guide for instance appear to you to be excessively cautious?*

3. *Discuss ways in which those who practise Christian healing can work alongside and in co-operation with orthodox medical practice. How do we get over the problem caused by there being so many different Christian groups with contrasting theological ideas?*

4. *Discuss ways in which social and political action affect the issues of health and healing. Identify ways in which certain political and social decisions could transform the health of people right across the world.*

5. *It has been said that death is the ultimate healing. What do you make of this?*

Salvation

John Bell and Graham Maule of the Iona Community have written and published some exciting conversations between Jesus and Peter. (*Eh Jesus, Yes Peter*, Wild Goose Publications). In one of them which is entitled 'Sophistication', Peter suggests that Jesus is not very sophisticated in that he does not use many long words such as Pentateuch, and does not talk about himself as Messiah or the Redeemer. He then adds another word which he suggests Jesus does not use – 'Salvation.' Here Jesus corrects him and refers to the occasion when he visited the home of Zacchaeus, the tax collector. Peter acknowledges his mistake and they discuss the incident when Jesus had formed a friendship with Zacchaeus which had some remarkable results, including Zacchaeus giving back their money to the people from whom he had extracted it.

Jesus then explains that if he began a new relationship by using religious jargon then this would set up a barrier between them. However, in this incident with Zacchaeus he had rejoiced in what had happened and felt that it was worthy to be called an experience of 'salvation'. It was not however the word which led to the experience; it was the experience which had led to his use of the word.

Many Christians, both young and old, would warm to this way of setting out our relationship with God through Jesus. There was a time when it was popular to set out God's plan of salvation in a somewhat mechanical way. First you had to accept your sinful state; then you had to confess your sins; this created a deep sense of sorrow which could be alleviated by the good news that Jesus had paid the price of our sin. God's need for justice had thus been satisfied and as individuals believed this to be true so they were saved. This was how salvation came about.

Many people, however, have found faith in God through Christ via a different route. They were attracted by the person of Jesus and they were both challenged and helped by becoming part of a vital Christian community. Like Zacchaeus they had shared in the experience without at first giving it a name. Then in some way this vital truth dawned. They were the friends of Jesus who had showed them the way, led them to the truth and shared with them his life. They had experienced salvation. The experience came before the doctrinal explanation.

Since that initial experience of being held by Jesus and through the company of his people, there have been other experiences of salvation proceeding throughout the whole of life. Salvation has been renewed in times of despair, difficulty and challenge. The normal process of growing up has provided many situations within which we have been saved.

The Bible text which provides this basis for this ongoing experience is:

> It is by God's grace that you have been saved through faith. It is
> not your own doing but God's gift.
>
> *Ephesians 2:8*

Let us now quietly meditate and pray as we are inspired by those key words . . .

Grace

The word *grace* means God's love in action directed towards me. Think of times when you have been especially aware of God's grace.

> Paul's ministry to his converts was *full of grace.*
> *from* Fare Well in Christ *by W. H. Vanstone*

We mediate God's grace by keeping our friendships in good repair. Grace is the enabling force behind acts of reconciliation. With whom do we need to be reconciled and have we asked for grace to take an initiative?

> O Lord my God, who has created me after thine own image and
> likeness, grant me this grace which thou hast shown me is so
> great and so necessary to salvation.
>
> *Thomas à Kempis*

Faith

Faith is born out of an awareness of the person of Jesus. It is not something we try to force. Sometimes we struggle for faith but in the midst of the struggles God often tells us to let go and rest in him.

> God desires our independence – which we attain when, ceasing
> to strive for it ourselves we fall back into God.
>
> *from* Markings *by Dag Hammarskjöld*

We are invited and summoned to take seriously the victory of God's glory in this man Jesus and to be joyful in him. Then we may live in thankfulness and not in fear.

from Dogmatics in Outline *by Karl Barth*

It was the *story* of particular events involving Jesus that the first preachers told and it was by the story that people were converted.

W. H. Vanstone referring to C. H. Dodd's
teaching in Fare Well in Christ

O Lord, give me saving faith; help me to trust in your gracious provision for my needs. Help me to move out of struggle into the rest which is your intention for me. As I let go so help me to turn to you in renewed and renewing trust.

The gift of God

The least that we may say, surely, is that God will never cease to desire and actively to work for the salvation of each created person. He will never abandon any as irredeemably evil. However long an individual may reject his maker, salvation will remain an open possibility to which God is ever trying to draw him.

from Evil and the God of Love *by John Hick*

I can on God implicitly rely;
he stands in all events my person by.
It's he whose love into my prison breaks,
who leads me out and makes my soul relax.

Fred Kaan, based on Psalm 23

O Lord, I accept your gift. I gratefully acknowledge that your heart's desire for me is that I should be saved and in a right and loving relationship with you and with my fellow human beings. I am aware that the consequence of accepting your love is to be loving and I would be spontaneous about this as I realise my need to avoid trying to earn your favour. So simply but meaningfully I say . . .

Thank you Lord, for saving my soul.
Thank you Lord, for making me whole.

2
Health and Healing:
A Biblical Exploration

If you have a concern about a particular aspect of the Christian faith there is always a strong temptation to turn to the Bible to discover books, passages and individual texts which underline and substantiate what has become your own vital interest. This often has the effect of your being selective in the choice of those parts of the Bible which support your case and at the same time paying scant attention to those which raise awkward questions. This temptation is certainly present in asking what the Bible has to say about health and healing issues. In this study we shall avoid building upon isolated verses and take the message of the Bible as a whole. Our theme throughout is to discover what the Bible teaches us about health, healing and wholeness and how this relates to the task of today's Church. Naturally we shall begin with the Old Testament because you cannot begin to grapple with many of the ideas and thought forms contained in the New Testament without reference to the Old. However, the basis upon which we build our considered belief in the validity of Christian healing ministry is Jesus himself. The Order of St Luke which is one of the organisations mentioned in the Introduction affirms the following statement:

> The New Testament clearly teaches that the healing of mind and body was a very real part of the total ministry of our Lord and that he commissioned his followers to continue this ministry.

So our ongoing concern will be to recognise that health, healing and wholeness are not peripheral ideas which some enthusiasts seek to advocate but a clear part of the message of the gospel which has to be taken seriously and acted upon through the regular ministry of the Church at every level.

Health and healing in the Old Testament

The creation stories emphasise that God did not create a passive people who would obey him automatically but a responsible people who could choose for themselves between obedience and disobedience. Those who obeyed would experience Shalom, a rich and expressive word which means much more than peace (which is the usual translation) as the absence of war, or inward contentment. It was a dynamic word which had to be experienced. I express some of its characteristics in an acrostic:

> Soundness
> Harmony
> Adaptability
> Love
> Oneness
> Movement

☞ *Think of a person who seems to display the characteristics of Shalom.*

The recipe for sharing in the Shalom experience is expressed as follows:

> If only you will obey the Lord your God, if you will do what is right in his eyes; if you will listen to his commands and keep all his statutes, then I shall never bring on you any of the sufferings which I brought on the Egyptians; for I the Lord am your healer.
>
> *Exodus 15:26*

It is interesting to note that the word 'obedience' is related to the word 'amen' which indicates consent and agreement.

The other Old Testament concept which is expressed through the word Shalom is the importance of corporate experience. Life is lived through relationships. One person may be expressing through a personal illness the breakdown of the life of a community. Such a person is technically known as a scapegoat. The relationships that matter are those with God, with ourselves, with our fellow community members and with the land. Thus another way of expressing the characteristics of those who enjoy the Shalom experience is that:

1. *They are seeking to relate to their creator God.*
2. *They are seeking to discover their own true selves.*
3. *They belong to a caring, understanding community.*
4. *They act responsibly towards God's created universe.*

Further evidence of this is to be found in the following verse:

> Righteousness will yield peace and bring about quiet trust for
> ever.
>
> *Isaiah 32:17*

But the exact opposite is possible:

> Why do you invite more punishment, why persist in your
> defection? Your head is all covered with sores, your whole
> body is bruised. From head to foot there is not a sound spot in
> you – nothing but weals and welts and raw wounds which
> have not felt compress or bandage or the soothing touch of
> oil.
>
> *Isaiah 1:5-6*

It is interesting to find how restoration is described in healing
terminology:

> But for you who fear my name the sun of righteousness will
> rise with healing in its wings.
>
> *Malachi 4:2*

☞ *Further aspects of Shalom understanding are to be found in individual
books of the Bible, particularly in the Prophets. Look up Hosea Chapter
11 and think about Redemptive Love. Look up Jeremiah 31 and think
about Inward Spirituality. Look up Isaiah Chapter 53 and think about
the Wounded Healer.*

So in much of the Old Testament there is a connection between sin
and sickness and an emphasis upon God punishing disobedience with
sickness and suffering. Obviously there is truth here for us for today
but not the whole truth. Innocent people do suffer and there is a mystery

about suffering which is tackled head on in the Book of Job. Job believed that his suffering was out of all proportion to any sin he had committed. He had sought to be obedient but the consequences had not been just. His so called friends were no comfort. They kept on saying the same thing in different ways. In the end Job did not get a satisfying intellectual resolution of his dilemma. He did, however, in Chapters 38-41, receive a marvellous vision of the glory and majesty of God's creation. Job was lifted into another world where his questions were no longer as important as once they were. He responded in trust and in faith when he said:

> I knew of you then only by report, but now I see you with my own eyes. Therefore I yield, repenting in dust and ashes.
>
> *Job 42:5-6*

God's righteousness, compassion and understanding are also underlined in some of the Psalms, especially Psalms 91 and 103.

So the main message of the Old Testament about health and healing can be summed up in our understanding of the deep meaning of the word Shalom. Of all the words we have used to fill out the meaning of the word Shalom the best is the word *wholeness.* So now we have a launching pad for the teaching, healing and preaching activity of Jesus.

☞ *Is the connection of sin with sickness still a valid concept? Think of cases which seem to demonstrate the link, then think of others which don't.*

Health and healing in the Gospels

The nature of the public ministry of Jesus was announced when he appeared in the Temple and read from the Book of the Prophet Isaiah:

> The spirit of the Lord is upon me, because he has anointed me; he has sent me to announce good news to the poor, to proclaim release for prisoners and recovery of sight for the blind; to let the broken victims go free, to proclaim the year of the Lord's favour.
>
> *Luke 4:18-19*

Combine with this the following description of his ministry and we get a picture of its comprehensiveness:

> He travelled throughout Galilee, teaching in the synagogues, proclaiming the good news of the Kingdom, and healing every kind of illness and infirmity among the people.
>
> *Matthew 4:23*

However, it is in keeping with our resolve to take the message of the Bible as a whole to note that, at times, the healing activities of Jesus proved to be a hindrance to his overall ministry. The late Archbishop Michael Ramsey made the following comment on this issue:

> We notice scenes where Christ deliberately avoids the crowds who came to him for healing. He healed – for his compassion overflowed; but we are not told that he sought the sick as he sought sinners.

The purpose of his coming was to proclaim that in his person the Kingdom had arrived. This offered to his hearers a total spiritual renewal which was something of far greater significance than a physical cure. The purpose of his coming was in order that people might

> believe that Jesus is the Christ, the son of God and that through this you may have life by his name.
>
> *John 20:31*

Notice now the different methods Jesus used to bring healing and wholeness to different people:

1. *He used the word of command (Mark 1:25, 5:8 and 9:25).*
2. *He touched people (Mark 6:5; Luke 4:40).*
3. *He used word and touch together (Matthew 8:3 and 9:29).*
4. *He used saliva (Mark 7:33-34, 8:23-25).*
5. *He healed at a distance (Matthew 8:13; Mark 7:29; John 4:50).*

But whatever method he used he awakened something within that sick person which opened them up to the activity of the Spirit of God which stimulated their own self-healing (God-given) energies, with positive consequences. His purpose, however, was always the same: to bring men and women into a saving relationship with God. This was their ultimate and proper healing and it was for this purpose Jesus came.

Some interesting statistics indicate that the healing aspect of the ministry of Jesus was always carried out in the context of preaching and teaching. There are thirty-eight accounts of healing recorded in the Gospels. Of these, twenty-six are concerned with individuals, and these can be divided into seventeen which relate to physical healing, six which refer to the casting out of demons, and three in which the dead are raised. It has been estimated that 50 per cent of Mark's Gospel is devoted to teaching, and 75 per cent of Matthew's Gospel. The amount of space devoted to healing in Matthew is around 9 per cent of the text and around 20 per cent in Mark. (These facts and figures are taken from *Health and Healing* by John Wilkinson, Handsel Press.)

So to sum up:

1. *Healings arose out of the compassion Jesus felt for needy people. They were an expression of his love.*

2. *Jesus was concerned that healing should be full and complete and part of a wider reconciliation; not just a restoration to function but a healing of the whole person.*

3. *Healing was facilitated by the relationship of trust established between Jesus and the needy person. Sometimes that trust and hope was provided by a third party (NB Trust = Faith).*

4. *Jesus did not usually seek publicity from his healings; indeed it was the opposite. He did, however, tell the Gadarene demoniac to tell his 'friends'. The Good News Bible has 'family'.*

5. *Even Jesus had his failures. 'He could do no mighty work there' (Mark 6:5).*

6. *Jesus sometimes used the primitive medicine of his day; i.e. spittle. (Oil and wine are also referred to in the Parable of the Good Samaritan.)*

7. *Jesus was reluctant to be thought of primarily as a healer and worker of miracles but he could not 'pass by on the other side'.*

☞ *Does your Church offer a balanced ministry to the community which includes preaching, teaching and healing?*

Health and healing in the Acts of the Apostles

The disciples were sent out by Jesus during the days of his flesh to

> proclaim the Kingdom of God and to heal the sick.
>
> *Matthew 10:5-10*
> *(see also Mark 6:7-13 and Luke 9:1-6)*

Later in the post-resurrection appearances of Jesus the commission to heal was not included in the final command to teach and to preach, to make disciples and to baptise:

> Full authority in heaven and on earth has been committed to me. Go therefore to all nations and make them my disciples; baptise them in the name of the Father, the Son and the Holy Spirit, and teach them to observe all that I have commanded you.
>
> *Matthew 28:18-20*

It has been suggested that this indicates that healing was only for the time of Jesus' public ministry and that when his authority as the Messiah had been established this aspect of ministry was no longer necessary. The disciples, however, continued to exercise a healing ministry and a number of specific healing acts are well documented. Peter was the instrument used in the healing of the lame man at the gate of the temple (Acts 3:1-10) and the healing of the paralysed Aeneas (Acts 9:32-5). Ananias was used to enable Paul to recover his sight (Acts 9:17-19). Paul was used to heal the cripple at Lystra (Acts 14:8-11); the father of Publius (Acts 28:8) and to exorcise demons from the Philippian slave girl (Acts 16:16-24). There are also references to the dead being raised through Peter in Acts 9:36-41 and through Paul in Acts 20:9-12. There are other general references which include the healing of groups. Acts 5:15-16 is one instance but there are at least three others.

It is, however, true that the number of references to actual healings in the Acts of the Apostles was reduced to 4.5 per cent of the total in terms of verses. The reasons for this can only be surmised. The major reason may well be, as was suggested above, that there was no longer any need to use healing miracles to convince people of the fact that Jesus was indeed the Christ. So the healings recorded were, in all probability, representative of many others.

Health and healing in the epistles

The most important of the records of healing in the epistles is Paul's own story in 2 Corinthians 12. The real significance of this story is that it is not an account of a physical healing. Paul wanted to be healed of his 'thorn in the flesh' but that did not happen in the way he hoped at first. Instead he was given the grace to live with his affliction and to discover the sufficiency of God's grace to meet his deepest needs. His experience has been the source of inspiration and comfort to countless numbers of those who have struggled with their afflictions.

The other reference of importance in St Paul's letters is in 1 Corinthians 12:4-11 and later in the same chapter verses 27-31. This is the statement about the gift of healing. This gift (charisma) is one among other gifts and it is not given to everyone. It is a mistake to think of the gift of healing as purely and only a supernatural gift whilst ignoring the seemingly natural gifts of empathy, discernment and understanding. The gift of healing is both natural and supernatural. There are those who seem to be able to help people more than others by virtue of an endowment which has been given to them in a vital and special way. There are those who insist that this is due to the way an individual's spiritual make-up has been given and that this gift is given to some who do not name the name of Jesus. It is interesting to observe the conclusion of a lay person with no Christian commitment who embarked upon a study of healing in many parts of the world.

> Healing is a miraculous phenomenon and one of mankind's greatest gifts. To me, the one continuous thread that wove together all the good healers I met was their capacity for unconditional love.
> – *from* I Fly out with Bright Feathers *by Allegra Taylor*

There are those who help others through a basic natural goodness which seems to work in spite of them being part of a sinful, unredeemed humanity. Some may want to question the ultimate good achieved. I believe that when that gift is offered back to God and used in the name of Jesus it is more efficacious in that there can be a total healing of body, mind and spirit, but I would not want to deprive another of receiving a good gift because it is offered with love but not in a recognised way in the name of Jesus. Our Lord himself did not condemn those who were not authorised to work in his name (Luke 9:49-50). Similarly the natural gifts of tenderness, compassion, and discernment can have vital healing consequences. The Holy Spirit works in many different ways and through many different channels. I prefer to rejoice when true healings *of any kind* take place through medicine, surgery, psychotherapy, prayer, the laying on of hands, anointing, together with the exercise of caring love. All that is good and wholesome is of God and to him be the glory.

There is a verse in the Epistle of James which bears specifically upon our subject. Here it is:

> Is one of you ill? Let him send for the elders of the church to pray over him and anoint him with oil in the name of the Lord; the prayer offered in faith will heal the sick man, the Lord will restore him to health, and if he has committed sins they will be forgiven.
>
> *James 5:14-15*

The emphasis here is upon the Church as a healing community. It is not an individual with a special gift who is to be sent for but the elders, the representatives of the Christian fellowship. There is also the association of healing with forgiveness. Confession to one another and prayer for one another has vital healing consequences. This is the normal, everyday work of the local Church.

☞ *In what ways is your Church being obedient to the clear instructions contained in James 5:14-15?*

The place of faith in the healing process

Our understanding of this difficult area has important implications for the ways in which we exercise pastoral care of those who are ill and also of those who are concerned for them. There are a number of healing stories in the New Testament where the sentence, 'your faith has saved you, go in peace', is used. Taking doctor Luke's Gospel as our starting point, the stories are:

1. *The woman described as a sinner at the house of Simon the Pharisee (Luke 7:36-50). Note that this was not a physical healing.*

2. *The servant of the centurion (Luke 7:1-10).*

3. *The blind beggar at Jericho (Luke 18:35-43, but also see Matthew 20:29-34).*

4. *The woman with a long-standing issue of blood (Luke 8:43-48, but also see Mark 5:25-34).*

So in addition to the four references in St Luke's Gospel, this key sentence is also used twice in St Mark's Gospel and once in St Matthew's. Note that some translations replace 'saved you' by 'made you well'. Both are legitimate translations of the Greek verb *sozo*.

Overall Luke reports twenty-four episodes of Jesus healing; six are general references to healings having taken place whilst eighteen are about specific individuals. In eight of these stories faith is mentioned as a significant factor. (I owe this information to Lindsey P. Pherigo's book *The Great Physician*, Abingdon Press.) On the basis of these references we can see that faith is an important factor in the healing activities of Jesus but its importance must not be over-exaggerated.

Thus all who are involved in the ministry of healing must never suggest that a person who is seeking help must have enough faith in order to be healed. Nor must we fall into the error of attributing so called failure to a person's lack of faith, either that of the person whose healing is being sought or that of the person seeking to be used as God's instrument.

What then is this faith which makes us whole?

1. *It is confidence in a group of people who commend themselves to you by their warmth, integrity, genuineness and humanity. The atmosphere of love and trust thus created may result in one of their number being appointed to act as the channel of ministry but it is with the authentic support of the whole group that they function.*

2. *It includes a belief in, and commitment to, the person of Jesus as he is to be discovered in the pages of the New Testament through the stories he told and the acts he performed.*

3. *This gives rise to an acute sense of awareness that it is in a relationship with Jesus that I can discover my true self.*

No one has put it better than Canon Frank Wright in his book, *The Pastoral Nature of Healing* (SCM Press):

> Faith means that I still myself, resting in the conviction that in God there is such a power of love as is sufficient for all my needs. I put myself in his hands without wishing to force any outcome or necessarily believing that I know best what that outcome should be. Again I go with the situation, not out of resignation, but because of my deep knowledge that I am held by him. That faith is as necessary and relevant . . . on the night before a surgical operation as when I am in a healing service. Faith is not something I manufacture by will-power and determination; it can only be the fruits of those periods of stillness, reflection, sacramental union, closeness to Jesus who always stands by me, who is always with me. In other words it is a quality which is tested in the ordinary experiences of life.

☞ *How do you help those who have been told that they lacked faith and therefore have not been cured?*

Questions for personal written answers or to promote discussion

1. *Explain how you would attempt to communicate the meaning and pastoral significance of the word 'Shalom'. (If in a group use this as the basis for discussion and build up the points of a corporate answer.)*

2. *Jesus seemed able to heal people of any kind of illness almost immediately. Why can't we do the same?*

3. *How do you explain the part played by faith in the healing process?*

4. *Discuss Paul's experience in 2 Corinthians 12:1-10 in the light of the following statement by Dr Michael Wilson: 'To be healthy is to be able to respond in a mature way to life as it is.'*

Words for Thought, Prayer and Meditation

Shalom

Those of you who have been to Israel will be familiar with the Shalom greeting. It is almost the equivalent of our 'good morning' or 'hello'. The usual basic understanding of the word is 'peace'. However, many Jews who use the greeting as a matter of course do not appreciate its full meaning. Shalom Peace is much more than the absence of war, or peace as tranquillity. It is a dynamic word which communicates an experience. That experience is characterised by additional words which fill it out; explore its deeper meaning. If you then go on to allow Shalom to be percolated by the life and love of Jesus you begin to appreciate its grandeur. It is the forerunner of another word which we shall often find in these pages – *wholeness*.

To unpack this word can be, in itself, a healing experience. In this act of devotion we are going to utilise the acrostic method. Each letter of the word shalom will open up to us another word which will provide a window into its deeper meaning.

S is for soundness

A piece of fruit may be described as sound when it is good throughout. No bruises; no dark centre where over-ripe fruit is going bad. Wholesome, mature, tasty, bringing the palate to life.

Two friends who died had these words spoken about them. The first was described as being *all of one piece*. Of the second it was said that she was *complete*.

Dwell on those two descriptions; remember Paul and his divided self in Romans 7, when he could not do what he wanted to do and did those things he didn't want to do. Then see the transformation in Romans 8.

> There is no condemnation for those who live in union with Christ Jesus.
>
> *Romans 8:1*

Now Paul is experiencing Shalom. He is being made whole. He is moving towards being *all of one piece*. He is on the road to *completion*.

H is for harmony

When we think of harmony our minds turn towards music. We think of notes which blend together. But musically harmony is more than that. In counterpoint for instance, a host of different individual melodies make their own tune but they all relate to each other. There are different sides to our individual personalities. Christians are in the process of finding themselves through finding God who has been made known to us in Jesus. Inner harmony may break down but if we refer ourselves back to Jesus it can be re-discovered.

In music dissonant notes have a part to play. The dark side of us, when better understood, can actually enrich our lives. A bad temper may, when it is out of control, damage both ourselves and others. When it is put under the constraints of Jesus it may be transformed into a creative energy with positive results.

> Jesus, harmonious name!
> It charms the hosts above;
> They evermore proclaim
> And wonder at his love.
> 'Tis all their happiness to gaze,
> 'Tis heaven to see our Jesu' face.
> *Charles Wesley*

A is for adaptability

As life goes on various changes take place – some of them sudden and unwanted, some of them gradual and anticipated. How do we adapt towards illness for instance? Peter Nixon, a consultant cardiologist, tries to get his patients to see that heart attacks are often related to lifestyle. Medical care can do so much but greater self-awareness is called for. He tries to help his patients to adapt and re-orientate their lives by discovering the ability to relax and find inner quietness. After an illness episode we can never just go back to being the kind of people we were. We have moved on and illness can be part of the educative process.

Ageing awaits most of us – or is a recognisable feature of our present experience. The ability to adapt to this stage of life is a challenge in itself. Here is how one person describes it:

A long life makes me feel nearer truth, yet it won't go into words, so how can I convey it? I can't and I want to. I want to tell people approaching and perhaps fearing age that it is a time of discovery. If they say – of what? I can only answer that we must each find out for ourselves, otherwise it won't be discovery.

anonymous

O Lord, help me to adapt to all the changing scenes of life and help me to transform life's negative experiences into positive voyages of discovery.

L is for love

In the Bible God is searching for all us human beings and, if we are wise, we are engaged in searching for God. There is one truth which is central to our Christian faith but other faiths share it as well. It is that *love desires the best for the objects of love.* A Christian pilgrimage is a journey in which one is moving towards understanding and accepting this truth. The only way we demonstrate that we have made it part of our lives is by loving others.

> I say for certain
> that before ever he made us,
> God loved us;
> and that his love
> has never slackened,
> nor ever shall.
> In this love,
> all his works have been done,
> and in this love,
> he has made everything serve us.
> And in this love
> our life is everlasting.
> Our beginning was when we were made,
> but the love in which he made us
> has never had beginning.
> *Julian of Norwich*

Love transforms. Love makes empty hearts overflow. This happens even more when we have to struggle through, without assurance, all unready for the play of love. *Mechtilde of Magdeburg*

Grant, O Lord, that none may love Thee less this day because of me, that never a word or act of mine may turn another soul from Thee. And ever daring, yet one other grace would I employ: that many souls this day, because of me, may love Thee more.

A medieval prayer

O is for oneness

The psychologists speak of integration. The different parts of us growing up and discovering how to live with each other. We have already explored a musical theme in our consideration of the word 'harmony', but we did not mention the one who conducts an orchestra or choir. The one who holds every instrument and voice together. Integration needs some kind of unifying principle. We have this *in Christ*.

Did you know that this phrase 'in Christ' occurs 169 times in Paul's letters? It might be described as his 'magnificent obsession'. Here is how the poet William Wordsworth describes having an overwhelming, unifying experience:

> . . . that serene and blessed mood,
> In which the affections gently lead us on –
> Until, the breath of this corporeal frame
> And even the motion of our human blood
> Almost suspended, we are laid asleep
> In body, and become a living soul:
> While with an eye made quiet by the power
> Of harmony, and the deep power of joy,
> We see into the life of things.
>
> *from 'Lines above Tintern Abbey'*

> Our prayer is God's work, God's creation.
> As you kneel there,
> sit there, walk about
> or whatever you do when you pray,
> you are saying yes with your whole being
> to his will that you should be,
> that you should be you,
> that you should be united in Him.
>
> *Maria Boulding OSB*

M is for movement

The exciting thing about the life of discipleship is that it enables constant movement in a God-ward direction. Another word for this might be growth. There is no sadder sight than a churhgoer who is constantly looking backwards. For them, if it's old it's good; if it's new, it's bad. Christ leads us into a life which is characterised by new opportunities, 'new mercies each returning day'. The truly remarkable thing about the Bible is that, though its stories and its individual words have been preached about and commented on millions and millions of times, it still retains its ability to move and inspire each one of us. When Alan Dale wrote *New World – The Heart of the New Testament in Plain English* (OUP), he declared in his preface:

> I have found the making of this translation an exhilarating experience. Putting the New Testament into simple language has forced me to reconsider my own Christian convictions and to see the plain story of what happened in a fresh light. I hope the reader will catch something of the excitement and enlargement I felt.

> When as a child I laughed and wept – time crept,
> When as a youth I dreamed and talked – time walked,
> When I became a full grown man – time ran.
> And later, as I older grew – time flew.
> Soon I shall find while travelling on – time gone.
> Will Christ have saved my soul by then? Amen.
>
> *Chester Cathedral*

> Shalom, Shalom, the gift of God above,
> The gift of peace and joy and light and love.
>
> Lord, give us peace, the peace that makes us whole,
> The peace that fills the heart and mind and soul.
>
> Lord, give us joy, the joy that comes from Thee,
> Found in completeness and security.
>
> Lord, give us life, the life from God above,
> Wholeness of being, blessedness and love.
>
> Lord, give us love, the love that sets us free,
> To work for others and to live for Thee.
>
> Shalom, Shalom, God's gift is thus assured –
> They shall find peace who wait upon the Lord.
>
> *from* Seven Whole Days *by Ivor Pearce*

3
Prayer and Healing

The big questions facing us in this study are – *does praying for sick people make any difference to them? Does prayer promote healing?*

Yes, I realise that it all depends upon what you mean by healing and this issue will be tackled later in this study, but we all know what is in the minds of those who ask this question. *Does praying have any effect upon the recovery rate of those for whom we pray? Does it help to bring about a cure?*

Here is a practical situation to focus this issue. A brother minister's daughter who was in the later stages of pregnancy suffered a subarachnoid haemorrhage (bleeding from a brain blood vessel). Immediately she was surrounded by a veritable barrage of prayer and vigils were held during the times when it was known that she would be undergoing surgery. In addition to prayer there was a great deal of practical help. The outcome was all that could be desired. First the baby was delivered whilst the mother was still unconscious. Then in due time delicate brain surgery released the pressure and allowed Jane's (not her real name) natural healing powers to take over. She was fully restored.

Naturally there was much rejoicing and thanksgiving and Jane was made to feel very special. Later, however, two other people, one a minister colleague, were taken ill with cancer. The same people prayed for them both with all the urgency and fervour previously mustered on behalf of Jane, but the end result was different. In both cases they died leaving sorrowing families.

These experiences meant that a considerable pastoral and theological dilemma was left in the minds and hearts of the many people who were at the centre of these events. The big question we asked in the opening sentence of this study was now a practical issue which had to be wrestled with in the situation itself. Jane was troubled by the way in which her recovery had been described as a miracle but the miracles which had been sincerely asked for from God in the other two cases were not repeated. The many questions asked by ordinary, sincere Christians prompted the minister concerned to take all the issues involved as the basis of a sabbatical study, to which the present writer is greatly indebted. These were some of the questions people asked.

1. *Why do some people who are prayed for recover and others do not?*

2. *Does the number of people who pray for individuals make any difference?*

3. *How can we rejoice and praise God in one instance and just fail to understand in another?*

4. *How do you decide between the part played by medical interventions, the operation of one's natural self-healing resources, and direct divine action?*

5. *How do you give pastoral support to those whose expectations have been stimulated by apparent success in one instance but who are deeply disappointed when the same does not happen in the case of their own loved ones?*

☞ *Work through each of the above questions and try to decide how, at this stage in your thinking, you would answer them.*

Begin here

The basis from which we begin our investigation is of great importance. Could it be that this is to ask a primary and fundamental question – *what is the main purpose of prayer? Is it asking God for what we naturally and legitimately desire?*

There are actually two questions here but they are intimately related. Let me begin by sharing a personal experience. I only really began to pray with any sense of release or true meaning when I stopped using a lot of words and sought to practise the presence of God. I found great help and support from a religious community who helped the activist, which I am by nature, to endeavour to discover quiet within myself. As I tried to get into touch with 'the still point of the turning world', to use T. S. Eliot's vivid phrase, God came alive for me in more meaningful ways. My life was enriched and I began to see things differently. I didn't have to rely on getting specific answers to requests to make me aware that prayer was important to me and to all my relationships.

Now I want to paint a word picture for you and invite you to put yourself inside the frame. In fact the picture is based on reality but on several relationships I have been privileged to enjoy.

I was put under someone's authority and after a little while began to enjoy the relationship greatly because it became clear that the person concerned saw me as an individual who mattered. The natural consequence was that I began to trust him and then, as the relationship deepened, trust turned to love and close bonds were formed between us. Then a particular situation arose in which I needed help. I asked him for help and that help was given in such a way that was greatly to my advantage. I was grateful and expressed my gratitude to him. Later another situation arose, not dissimilar to the first but not exactly the same. Again I went for help to the one I trusted who had been the means of helping me before. This time his response was different. He took me aside and told me that he did not think it right to help in exactly the way I wanted but that he would be with me in the complications arising from this particular dilemma and I could go to him at any time for advice and support. I accepted the situation and sought to work things out by making my own decisions. The result was that I grew up a little and our relationship was even deeper than before.

This leads me to give a direct answer to the primary question as to the purpose of prayer, which is, to quote a perceptive writer, Neville Ward, 'that we might know God and love him and do his will' (*The Use of Praying*, Epworth Press, now op). Another way to describe the primary purpose of prayer is to turn to the Westminster Confession where we read that 'the chief end of man is to enjoy God and glorify him for ever and ever'.

Does this mean that we should never pray for those about whom we are concerned with the object in mind that the sick should be made whole? Certainly not. Experience and testimony affirm that prayer and ministry directed to those who are sick makes a profound difference to their ultimate health and well-being. In addition we have the wealth of biblical evidence which we have already examined to some extent but which we shall certainly look at again in this chapter.

What it does mean is that we should never go to God with requests that his response should be exactly as we desire and that this and no other response will do. Look back to the word picture we painted above and let it speak to you again.

☞ *Have you felt disappointed by the consequences of your own 'asking' prayers? Do you feel that your faith has been strengthened or diminished by what has happened?*

How then are prayer and healing related?

To try to answer this question is to skirt around the edges of mystery but it is a natural human desire to seek answers to questions which are of such vital importance. Many have wrestled with this issue and have come up with a variety of explanations, none of which seems to me to offer the final answer but each of them is worthy of consideration.

1. *The somewhat brutal suggestion is sometimes made that those for whom healing is sought but not found are not living within the will of God.*

2. *We must always add to our prayers for healing the codicil 'not my will but thine be done' – and in many cases it is not God's will to respond in the way we ask.*

3. *God is sovereign and we must not question how he responds to our prayers. This is part of the mystery of God's nature into which we must not probe.*

☞ *Do any of the above explanations appeal to you? Take them one by one and make your own response.*

Are there other clues?

I believe there are and I believe that they harmonise more readily with our analysis of the primary purpose of prayer.

1. *Schweitzer and Jung used the phrase 'the inner doctor' to describe the person's own natural healing resources. It is these natural powers which both physicians and surgeons seek to release when they are treating*

their patients. Prayer and ministry add another dimension which is just as significant. To utilise this dimension is to make a valuable contribution to the healing process.

2. *We have already referred to the perceptive lecture given by the Revd Tom Smaile to the annual meeting of the Churches' Council on Health and Healing in 1992 (Chapter 1). This was to the effect that in the act of creation God established natural laws which are seldom by-passed but instead God affirms and perfects his own laws and utilises and enhances them by making fresh contact available through prayer and ministry. This combines with the God-given blessings of medicine and surgery to bring to life 'the inner doctor' (see above) which acts when order has broken down in illness. This healthy combination, when communicated by a dedicated humanity, brings together those sundered parts in a greater wholeness that is healing. In that process love plays a vital part. His other point about the consequences of prayer and ministry emphasises that healing through the forgiveness of sins is not always accompanied by physical improvement. The age factor has always to be borne in mind. I am reminded here of a note left for me by an American minister with whom I had been exchanging churches one summer. Describing a gracious Christian man who was suffering from a debilitating illness he referred to him by name and wrote: 'He is the healthiest sick person I have ever met.'*

☞ *How do you respond to the idea that the forgiveness of sins is more readily available than a recognisable act of healing – physical, mental, emotional or spiritual?*

Another look at the biblical material

Although no consideration of the biblical material could ever be considered as adequate, it has, I believe been reasonably summarised in the previous chapter, to which I re-direct your attention. Here I try to pick out the salient features as they particularly apply to the relationship between prayer and healing.

There are a number of separate verses in the New Testament which, if taken in isolation, suggest that God always answers our prayers in the ways in which we ask:

> Ask and it shall be given you, for one who asks always
> receives.   *Matthew 7:7-11 and Luke 11:9-13*

> I tell you solemnly . . . if two of you agree to ask anything at
> all it will be granted by my Father in heaven.
>   *Matthew 18:19*

Such promises taken literally and applied to recovery from illness
brook no equivocation yet we know from experience that it does not
seem to work out that way and in any case there are other passages of
scripture that give another side of the picture. Look at the following:

> To everybody he said, 'Anyone who wants to be a follower of
> mine must renounce self; day after day he must take up his
> cross and follow me.'   *Luke 9:23*

> Discipline, to be sure, is never pleasant; at the time it seems
> painful, but afterwards, those who have been trained by it
> reap the harvest of a peaceful and upright life.
>   *Hebrews 12:11*

Paul's experience has already been referred to briefly in the previous
chapter but it is vital to our understanding of the relationship
between prayer and healing. Of his own illness, which he described as
a 'thorn in the flesh', he wrote:

> Three times I begged the Lord to rid me of it, but his answer was
> 'My grace is all you need; power is most fully seen in weakness.'
>   *2 Corinthians 12:8 and onwards*

In addition some of Paul's fellow workers are described as being sick –
Epaphroditus and Trophimus for instance. Timothy was told to:

> Stop drinking only water; in view of your frequent ailments
> take a little wine to help your digestion.
>   *1 Timothy 5:23*

Perhaps the biblical equivalent of a Rennie or Milk of Magnesia
tablet!

However, it is vital that we examine the question of whether the suffering to which Jesus referred in the disciple's obligation to take up his or her cross, refers to illness at all, or rather more specifically to persecution. Was it this kind of suffering Paul also refers to when he wrote:

> My one desire is to know Christ and the power of his resurrection, and to share his sufferings.
>
> *Philippians 3:10*

The suffering endured in sickness is always to be fought. Suffering through illness is not the primary will of God for his children. The disciples were sent out to preach, to teach and to heal. The whole object of their mission was to enable a greater health and wholeness to be discovered. The 1920 report from the bishops of the Anglican communion put this in the strongest possible terms:

> Health is God's primary way for his children, and disease is not only to be combated, but combated in God's name as a way of carrying out his will.

Having established this as God's primary purpose nevertheless we know that people who have faith, and those who don't, do suffer through illness, sometimes in terrible ways. Of course much illness and disease in the world is due to our own misuse and abuse of our bodies and minds and of God's creation, but there will always remain the dilemma encountered by Job referred to in our biblical exploration. From time to time we are faced with mystery.

It is then, however, that God's will *in the circumstances* begins to operate and here Paul's experience with his 'thorn in the flesh' is vital to our understanding. As we have already seen, in this instance God did not deliver Paul from his illness but he was with him in a very special way *within* his illness. Thus he was able to triumph over his inward circumstances and, it would seem, grow as a person himself; since then he has enabled many people to share his experience of God's grace being sufficient.

Refer back to the words of Jesus quoted early in this study about God responding immediately to our requests (see Matthew 7:7-11 and John 14:13 especially). We know that Jesus, on other occasions, used the language of hyperbole in order to give emphasis to the point he was making. Like 'the camel through the eye of a needle' for instance. He needed to stress the vital importance of believing prayer but faith was never to be seen as guaranteeing that our every request would be met. The other verses we have looked at help us to get a more rounded picture of the relationship between prayer and healing.

☞ *Just how would you encourage a friend who seeks your help to receive a ministry of prayer, the laying on of hands and anointing?*

The prayer of faith

The biblical evidence has been examined in the previous chapter but the subject of this chapter requires that we look again at the issues involved primarily for pastoral reasons.

The simplistic statement that God's apparent reluctance to bring healing in certain cases is due to (a) a lack of faith on the part of the sick person, or (b) a lack of faith on the part of those who are offering prayer and ministry, has often been a most damaging comment and has led to much mental and emotional suffering, not to mention theological confusion. We have already seen that in the New Testament records faith is stated to be an ingredient in the healing process but not all the time and not in every instance recorded. (See John 5:2-16 for instance. The man at the Pool of Bethesda did not even know who Jesus was.)

I have found two comments on this dilemma to be particularly helpful. The first is by J. Motyer in *The Message of James* (Inter Varsity Press). Referring to the promises of healing in response to faith he writes:

> . . . the one thing the promises do not encourage or allow is that we should come into the place of prayer in a stubborn insistence that we have got it right and that our will must be done . . . In the prayer of faith it is not that the 'promises' will be fulfilled just like that; it is the faith which rests trustfully in the sovereign, faithful and loving God.

The second is by John Richards in *Faith and Healing*.

> Do not try to manipulate God in the guise of having faith in
> him. Faith is not getting God to give his attention to what we
> are focusing on, but giving our attention to what he is focusing
> on.

☞ *Look back at the quotation from Canon Frank Wright in* The Pastoral
Nature of Healing *included in the previous chapter and see if it reinforces
the quotations above.*

What do we mean by 'healing'?

There remains one issue to be faced as was indicated right at the
beginning of this chapter: *What do we really mean by the word 'healing'
in a direct Christian context?*

It has often been pointed out that healing embraces a much wider
concept than cure. Cure is often understood as meaning a return to
the state we were in before we became ill, i.e. the illness symptoms have
been removed; taken out of the experience of the person concerned.
This is a simplification in itself because no person remains the same
after a particular illness episode, particularly a serious, life-threatening
one. Healing, however, may include cure but it is primarily about the
development and growth of a human person. It is about moving
towards a greater harmony of body, mind and spirit. It is a learning
process in which we grow closer to God and are in receipt of his grace
and aware of his love. It enables a person to become one who is able to
face up to the realities of life, be they sickness or health, in a mature
way. To quote Jurgen Moltmann's definition of health, it is:

> the strength to live, the strength to suffer, and the strength to
> die. Health is not a condition of my body, it is the power of
> my soul to cope with varying conditions of that body.
> *from* The Power and the Powerless

To be healed then is to become the kind of person Moltmann
describes, but such are the ways of divine grace that this always does
mean positive changes in one or other of physical, mental, emotional
and spiritual health, and often in a combination of several of the qualities

mentioned. God's grace is a many splendoured thing which human experience confirms has a variety of consequences. We are truly healed when we can accept those consequences in love and humility, knowing that, in Paul's words, 'Faith, hope and love abide for ever – and the greatest of these is love.'

What is the way forward?

1. *We should certainly pray for the sick in accordance with James 5:14. It should be the whole person we pray for and sometimes the consequences may be wider and more comprehensive than we anticipate.*

2. *We should pray in trusting faith but not make the mistake of confusing our desires and God's will.*

3. *When we pray for the sick we are loving them in Jesus. Leslie Weatherhead used to tell his congregation that they were activating the collective unconscious. This was the channel God was using to link the corporate love of the congregation with the needs of those for whom prayer was being offered.*

4. *As medicine, surgery, counselling and psychotherapy are all directed towards facilitating the person's own healing and recuperative powers, so are our prayers and their importance must not be played down.*

5. *When we pray for the sick we are privileged to become fellow workers with God. This is of inestimable benefit to all concerned.*

6. *We should always pray for the sick intelligently by giving time and close attention to the task.*

7. *Prayer can often be combined with ministry such as the laying on of hands and anointing and we should always consider the possibility of utilising those to whom God seems to have given the gift of healing.*

Questions for personal written answers or to promote discussion

1. *Harold Taylor suggests in* Sent to Heal *(Order of St Luke, Australia) that because of the negative ideas which may accompany using the words 'if it be thy will' we use a form of words such as 'Lord, heal this person and make him/her whole in the way that you would have him/her be.' How do you respond to this? Discuss the words we use when praying for healing and ministering to sick people. How can you be both positive and yet not, at the same time, arouse false hopes?*

2. *We have said that illness is always to be fought but we have also implied that it can be a discipline to promote spiritual growth. How do you reconcile these two concepts?*

3. *A professional health worker (doctor, nurse, etc.) in your congregation says to you, 'Leave healing the sick to us; this is a job for the professionals.' How would you answer them?*

4. *How important is 'the inner doctor' concept in the healing process? Respond to Tom Smaile's ideas about God's natural laws being reinforced and activated by prayer and ministry.*

Trinity in Unity

And now glorious and blessed God, Father, Son and Holy Spirit, you are mine and I am yours.

from the Methodist Covenant Service

The individual exists on many levels. These include the physical, the mental and emotional, and the spiritual. All of them are equally important in achieving health. None is 'more real' than any other.

from Holistic Health *by Dr Lawrence Le Shan*

So faith, hope, love abide, these three; but the greatest of these is love.

1 Corinthians 13:13

Magnified and praised be the living God; he is, and there is no limit to his time and being. He is One, and there is no unity like his unity; he is inconceivable and his unity is unending. He has neither bodily form nor substance: we can compare nothing to him in his holiness. He was before anything that has been created, even the first: but his existence has no beginning. Behold he is the Lord of the Universe; to every creature he teaches his greatness and his sovereignty.

from the Hebrew Prayer Book

The concept of Trinity in Unity is basic to our understanding of the nature of God. This is how God has come to us – as Father, Son and Holy Spirit. Difficult to understand and explain at the intellectual level, but a fact of experience.

Holistic medicine shows to us the importance of taking seriously the threefold nature of the human person. To concentrate exclusively upon physical health is a serious error and leads to a warped and unbalanced view of what it is to be truly healthy. This in its turn can generate internal conflicts which can adversely affect our total being.

At certain times and stages in life one aspect of being seems to become all-important: an illness; and emotional crisis; a loss of a faith which had previously seemed to be a vital part of our existence. It is important that we prepare for all such times by seeking to be aware of the whole. If we do so we are less likely to be drawn into the part when such difficult times overwhelm us. Once developed and practised, the other parts of the whole will become relevant when we need them most.

In this time of thought, prayer and meditation, I invite you to dwell upon another Trinity – that of Faith, Hope and Love. Move slowly and quietly through the brief expositions and suggestions for meditative prayer.

Faith

Many years ago a Christian surgeon friend inspired confidence in his patients by his caring understanding of their needs. He explained carefully what he hoped to be able to do for them and always pointed out that his contribution was to pave the way for the natural healing energies to do their work. To those he considered it appropriate he would share his own faith that God had given those natural healing resources. The result of this was that patients had faith in him and this made a difference in their recovery or in their attitude towards continued limitations and even death.

Think of someone you know and trust. A person in whom you have faith. Transfer that kind of trusting faith to God whom you cannot see or feel or touch but who you recognise in the face of Jesus. Use your imagination to see Jesus standing by you and laying his hands upon you. Listen to him as he assures you using the words of Isaiah 43:1:

> Do not be afraid for I have redeemed you, I have called you by your name, you are mine.

As we practise the consequences of faith – discipline, caring, giving so our inner faith increases and we feel more secure.

> I have been thinking much about God,
> about the essence of my life,
> and, as it seemed, only to feel doubtful
> as to both the one and the other;
> and I questioned the evidence of his existence.
> And then, not long ago,
> I simply felt the desire to lean myself
> upon faith in God,
> and in the imperishableness of my soul;

and to my astonishment
I felt such a firm assurance
as I had never felt before.
So that all my doubts and testings
evidently not only did not weaken,
but to an enormous extent confirmed, my faith.

from the writings of Leo Tolstoy

Forward be our watchword.
Author of faith, eternal word.
In heavenly love abiding.
Take my life and let it be.
Happy the souls to Jesus joined.

Lord, I do have some faith, as I turn my eyes towards Jesus I ask you to grant me a rich increase. I do believe, help me where my faith falls short.

Hope

Hope is concerned with what lies before us. It is deeply personal. It is natural to hope for the best especially if we are in a situation we dislike and would like to move forward into a new situation where the darkness is left behind. Hope is often specific: I hope to get better from my illness; I hope that the person I have come to love will return my love and that a deep and special relationship will ensue . . .

It can be profitable to transfer our hope from the specific to the general. To cultivate our hope in the promise that nothing can separate us from the love of God.

Faith gives substance to our hopes, and makes us certain of realities we do not see.

Hebrews 11:1

God gives grounds for hope in a loving relationship with Jesus which leads us on into life that cannot be destroyed by death (see John 3:16).

All my hope on God is founded;
He doth still my trust renew.
Me through change and chance he guideth,
Only good and only true.
God unknown,
He alone
Calls my heart to be his own.

Robert Bridges and Joachim Neander

A man lost a fortune in a stockmarket crash. He lived by the sea and decided to end it all by walking into the ocean. The waves were almost over his head when he felt a shell pressed into his hand. He stopped and looked at it and felt it. It was so slim and fragile. Why was it not broken by the powerful waves? He realised that this was because it was pliable. It bent to the pressures placed upon it; it absorbed them – and so survived.

He turned back to the shore. He looked into the mystery of life and saw new possibilities. 'I will begin again', he said to himself. 'I have hope.'

Lord, there are times when I feel lost and lonely. The future seems so uncertain. I am afraid. In times like these I ask you to inspire me with hope. Not just hope in anything but hope in Jesus who said that he was the 'resurrection and the life'. May I now rise with him to be possessed by a new and living hope.

Love

Love is of the very essence of God's being. 'God is love' (1 John 4:8). God's love for us comes first. Our love for him is then a response to his for us. But all this can seem so far away from our experience. It appeals to the mind but not to the heart. Often love is aroused within our hearts by the love of another human person. This opens us up and points the way to the source of all love – God himself.

The founder of the Samaritans, Chad Varah, was once approached by a man in need of help. The parson in him replied with a spiritual platitude: 'My friend, God loves you.' The man in need replied, 'That may well be but what I want to know is, do you love me, and if so what are you going to do about it?'

A fellow student years and years ago was not a very happy man. He always seemed to look upon the darker side of life but this was all changed when he fell in love. His whole personality was transformed. Love bore him up as though he was on eagles' wings. That love endured until he died – and throughout his life he helped many others to realise that they were loved by him who is the source of love – the living God.

Lord, you showed your love so wonderfully in Jesus, who for the joy that was set before him endured the cross, despising the shame.

Thank you.

Lord, I do feel that you love me and that your love is down to earth and practical. It points to my needs and then relates to them in specific and caring ways.

Thank you.

Lord, I ask you to guide me so that I may be able to share your love with others.

Please.

> God of love, give us love. Love in our thinking and our speaking; Love in our doing and in the hidden places of our souls; Love of our neighbours far and near. Love of those we find it hard to bear and of those who find it hard to bear with us. Love in joy. Love in sorrow. Love in life and love in death.
>
> *from the writings of William Temple*

4
The Church as a Therapeutic Community

In the sixties and seventies hospitals dealing with patients with mental and emotional problems began to talk about the therapeutic community. The idea was to create a community within the hospital comprising patients, staff, and in some cases patients' relatives. There would be greater openness and improved communication. It would not be the experts on one side of the table and the needy patients on the other. Both staff and patients had needs, albeit of different kinds. With greater honesty would come improved trust. The aim and objective was personal growth on the part of all concerned. With that growth would come greater self-awareness and that would be a vital factor in the total therapy being offered. Of course drug treatments and individual psychotherapy would go on side by side with new and improved relationships but there would be fuller explanation of their hoped-for effects and, in the case of drugs, greater honesty about possible side-effects. The therapeutic group was a vital element in this visionary regime. Patients met with staff in groups and explored each other's feelings and reactions. Staff abolished uniforms and informal dress became the order of the day.

The dream has faded somewhat although remnants remain. The therapeutic group is still widely used, as is art therapy and, in some hospitals, music therapy. Uniforms have not been reintroduced. Drug therapies have advanced and of course are much easier to utilise. In some hospitals there is still a willingness to experiment with better human relations and improved communication but the concept of the therapeutic community is no longer discussed as once it was.

In the New Testament it is interesting to note that there is a close relationship between the two verbs *therapeuo* – to heal and *sozo* – to save. The following are the definitions of the two words in Grimm's Lexicon of the New Testament in Greek and English: *Therapeuo* – to serve, to do service, to heal, to cure, to restore health. Whereas *sozo* has the following definitions: to save, to rescue, to make safe, to heal, to restore to health.

Therapeutic has become a word largely associated with medicine and the medical profession's activities, whilst salvation is a religious word related to theological understanding and spiritual activity. But the words are virtually interchangeable, suggesting that therapy taken in the widest sense has a spiritual dimension and that salvation as a religious experience has wider consequences than a purely spiritual experience; it has physical, mental and emotional consequences.

The importance of the spiritual dimension is being taken much more seriously today. 'As a person thinks in his heart so he is.' Attitudes towards illness are of vital importance in the recovery process. The acquiring of spiritual resources has therapeutic consequences. This calls for much greater co-operation between those who practise medicine and those who offer pastoral support based on spiritual insights. If there was greater unity between churches this would work through into the hospital situations and also into primary health care based on general practitioner activity. In some situations this does exist at the local level where relationships of trust have been established between doctors and hospital chaplains and local ministers and priests. A study by the Revd A. Ward Jones on this kind of co-operation has shown that the basic element is mutual trust. When those concerned know each other well and have faith in each other's professionalism, informal co-operation is possible and indeed is taking place in a variety of situations. (See 'A survey of general practitioners' attitudes to the involvement of clergy in patient care' which was published in *Psychological Perspectives on Christian Ministry,* Gracewing.)

One positive development I have noticed since ceasing to be a hospital chaplain and involved in various NHS committees is the high profile given to the role of hospital chaplains by many of the NHS Hospital Trusts. This is revealed in the advertisements for new appointments. The job description and the qualities required are often most encouraging.

☞ *What has all the above to say about the way we are functioning in our own local Churches? Have we properly explored the therapeutic consequences of our own Church-based activities? How is what is happening in your Church furthering the health and wholeness of those who attend?*

Is the local Church a therapeutic community?

The above question has invited you to begin your own explorations into this issue. Certainly the relationship between the Greek words *therapeuo* and *sozo* would suggest that this is a fact and where God, and the ministry of Jesus as revealed in the Bible, is taken seriously, then Christian experiences do have therapeutic consequences.

In inviting you to consider this question in relation to your own Church communities, then I must do the same. My reflections recall for me times when I was under heavy pressure in my job as a Church-based pastor. Trying to create a therapeutic community meant for me that I had to look to other forms of Christian community life to give me strength, inspiration and vision. I found this kind of help in a variety of ways but I want to mention three in particular.

The first was within an organisation which no longer exists, The Methodist Society for Medical and Pastoral Psychology. In the late fifties I attended a study course sponsored by the above organisation. The studies were certainly helpful both in my own self-awareness and also in my pastoral care but the main advantage was that I found myself in a group of about a dozen young men (these were the days before the ordination of women) who seemed to have similar needs to myself and who in that context and with wise leadership were able to share their own deepest needs. The group attending the study course became a therapeutic group. We were helped within ourselves but we were also given a vision of what we wanted our own churches to become.

Later I moved to another area and was able to begin a relationship with a Roman Catholic Women's Community known as The Grail. Two groups sponsored by that community were of tremendous help to me. First, a Friday evening meditation group used to meet for three-quarters of an hour in their lovely chapel. We were given a simple introduction to meditation using our own scripture sentence (mine was 'Be still and know that I am God'); some recorded music followed, and then we were still for thirty minutes until the music came on again and told us that our meditation was over. Secondly, a lunch group met, consisting of about six lay people, two clergy and the leader of the Grail Community. We enjoyed a simple lunch of soup and bread and cheese and then just shared with one another our own personal agendas. It was a tremendous source of release and from time to time my burdens were lifted.

Another move brought me near to a Franciscan Friary. Here I was able to share in their worship, use their library for study and meet with The Guardian, Brother Bernard at that time, for pastoral conversation. He helped me further along the way to a greater self-awareness which was linked to a greater sense of God-awareness.

These three experiences of Christian community life helped me to feel that *I was loved and accepted; that I could drop my mask and be my true self and that it was possible to find deeper quiet within myself. Out of these experiences true worship (thankfulness to God) flowed more naturally.*

I thus came to believe that ...

If the Church is to be a therapeutic community it must provide safe areas where people can be vulnerable

I was helping with a Church weekend conference in a residential centre. I was the visiting speaker and I did not know the Church nor any of its members. On the Saturday night the young minister told me after dinner that he felt led to announce that there would be a 'late night extra'. This was additional to the planned programme and no one was pressured into coming. At ten o'clock he arranged some armchairs around a low table on which stood a lighted candle. About fifteen people come and he then put out the main lights, placing us in semi-darkness. He explained that he had felt led to offer this opportunity for people to express anything which was on their minds. He hoped that it would be completely confidential and that some might feel led, from time to time, to also offer a short prayer. No one was to worry, however, about long periods of silence. He felt sure that, in the silence, God would speak to us individually.

Next to me sat a middle-aged lady who was obviously in the grip of a deep emotion. She was trembling and breathing deeply. Suddenly, out it came – betrayal by her former husband, leaving her with a small child (who seventeen years later was actually in that circle). The shame of the experience had burnt deep into her soul and so she had moved to a new area where she had begun to attend the Church whose conference she was sharing in that weekend. Her story was simply how that Church had helped her to rebuild her life and that of her daughter. Her gratitude just overflowed and many – including her daughter, now in her early 20s – were in tears. The sense of release then enabled others to share their experiences, and some short but meaningful prayers were offered.

Also present was a young married woman who had been drawn to that Church through the Wives' Club. We had spoken several times and on the Sunday morning we were both taking a dip in the pool. I don't know why I said to her what I did but I know that I felt led so to do. It was something like this: 'We are all leaving later today, Ruth, I've enjoyed our chats. I like you; you really are a lovely person.' That seemed to embarrass her and she swam away up the pool. That was our last conversation but when I got home I received a letter from her which, among other things, said: 'Thank you for saying that you liked me; it helped because I came to that weekend not liking myself very much. I have decided that I will try to express some of my feelings outwardly and not keep everything to myself.'

A poem by Matthew Arnold puts it so well:

> Only, but this is rare
> When a beloved hand is laid in ours,
> When, jaded with the rush and glare
> Of the interminable hours,
> Our eyes can, in another's eyes read clear.
> When our world-deafened ear
> Is by the tones of a love voice caressed –
> A bolt is shot backwards in the breast,
> And a lost pulse of feeling stirs again;
> The eye sinks inward and the heart lies plain;
> And what we mean, we say, and what we would, we know.
> A man becomes aware of his life's flow.

A therapeutic community is a healing community. Healing is not just about restoration to function; it is about the development of the whole person. Healing moves us on; it enables us to grow and to become more whole. Providing safe space for vulnerable people is a vital factor in this health- and life-giving process.

☞ *When did I last feel safe enough to open up to another person with thoughts and feelings about which I feel guilty or ashamed? Do I have a safe place to go to when I am ready to be the real me? If I felt that somebody else needed such a place would I be able to help them myself? Is there effective provision for meeting these needs in my Church?*

It follows on from this that . . .

A therapeutic community provides good listeners

So many people in our society today need someone to listen to them. Many doctors do not have time; Department of Health and Social Security Officers try to get rid of callers as quickly as possible. Good listeners are at a premium. If the Church is to be a therapeutic community it must take this task very seriously and be prepared to train people to become good and effective listeners.

Many of the qualities required for good listening are to be found in that wonderful meditation on love I first found in The Grail Community to which I have referred. Here are just a few extracts:

> Love is openness, commitment.
>
> Love is being available,
> helping, rendering a service.
>
> To love is to create space
> where the other can be himself/herself.
>
> Love is communication, partnership, exchange.
>
> To love is to encourage, to value, to give strength.
>
> Love is accepting the other as he/she is
> with their weaknesses and strengths.
>
> Love is warmth and life, goodness and sorrow,
> happiness and pain.
>
> To love is to become the other.
>
> *from* Tools for Meditation *by J. de Rooy*

☞ *Work your way through each extract separately and ask yourself how you can discover for yourself the experiences and abilities which undergird each one.*

There are many books which summarise the qualities required in a good listener. Such things as demonstrating warmth, being accepting, non-judgemental, showing respect, clarifying issues and summarising from time to time. Making sure that your questions are open-ended and do not invite *yes* and *no* answers. Most importantly listen for feelings and encourage their expression. Feelings are often more important than facts. Good training, however, will provide more than a series of hints and guidelines. These are important background but you need to get the feel of good listening by taking part in role-play exercises and being supervised by someone with experience. An organisation which provides courses in good listening is the Acorn Christian Healing Trust (see Introduction for address). Suitable books are *Listening* by Anne Long, published by Daybreak, and my own little study guide *Healing through Caring*, published by Arthur James.

Now we make a positive statement about the faith which undergirds the local Church as it functions in a therapeutic way . . .

A therapeutic community acts upon its basic beliefs

Many local churches would agree with a great deal of what has been written above but they do not actually act upon what they believe. The sick are prayed for and ministered to but often in perfunctory ways. That is why in this study course I have devoted a whole chapter to the question, *Does praying for sick people make any difference?* The Church where my wife and I are members has a weekly prayer group. Immediately after each meeting a card is despatched to each person who has been remembered in prayer. Prayer lists given to the minister conducting worship can often simply be a series of names that are read. Far better to spend time with each name giving simple details of their needs and using the corporate imagination of the whole congregation to set up a connecting link between the person being prayed for and the congregation engaging in prayer. Leslie Weatherhead, as we have already noted, used to quote Jung's phrase 'the collective unconscious' as providing the channel of communication we can use. The chapter mentioned above goes into this important area of Church life in much more detail.

It has often been said that all worship services are healing services and this is absolutely true. Nevertheless just as in the liturgical year special aspects of Christian truth are emphasised at particular times – Incarnation, Resurrection, Ascension, Gift of the Holy Spirit – so the healing activity of Jesus needs to be carefully considered and its implications for today's Church assessed and put into practice as one important aspect of Christian truth. Healing services are but one way of doing this and they can be of great help both to individuals with a variety of needs and to the Church communities sponsoring them. Their aim is to bring a greater wholeness into people's lives thus promoting greater integration and deeper inward harmony. The consequences can be wide and varied. From time to time there will be noticeable physical improvement; at other times relationships will be healed and deep forgiveness to each other extended between those who have quarrelled and ceased to communicate with one another. A minister had two ladies in his congregation who had not spoken to each other for years. He *arranged* for them to be placed next to each other at the rail at a Communion Service. Without asking their permission he laid one hand upon each of them and prayed; then he joined their hands together and blessed them. They left the rail to sit together and then make the reconciliation complete. Healing comes in so many different, but delightful ways.

The efficacy of touch is often underestimated. With love in our hearts we can convey vital spiritual energies to people in need. Even as I write I am seeking to do this with someone who has a very real need. The doctors and all their ancillary workers are playing their part. Equally we are seeking to do ours and to help this person to utilise better her own inward healing powers to which our prayers and our *touch* will, we believe, add power and effectiveness.

☞ *Have we any experience of the healing power of touch? Have you felt helped by another person touching you either as an expression of sympathy and understanding or as a sacramental act?*

Promoting serious thought about all these issues is vital. All too often those who are known to exercise a healing ministry will be called upon by a desperate relative of someone in a terminal state as being 'our last hope'. It is never too late to care for someone in need but it is so much better when the thinking has been done in advance of the crisis. A Scottish lady lay dying, and the minister asked her if he should pray for her. She declined his offer with great dignity and said: 'I thicket ma hoose when the weather was waarm' (I thatched my house in fine weather). This naturally brings us to the last point to be made about the positive nature of the Church being a truly therapeutic community.

A therapeutic community is open, honest and realistic about death

Canon Frank Wright in his splendid book *The Pastoral Nature of Healing* (SCM Press) suggests that we need to speak more about the fear of dying, the process of dying and the meaning of death. He shared his own experiences of standing at the gateway of death as an RAF navigator in the last war and then more recently of being in the grip of a coronary heart attack which later necessitated a triple by-pass operation.

Dr Gordon Rupp said that when he reached the age of sixty-three he suddenly realised that the next most important thing that was going to happen to him now was that he was going to die.

The hospice movement has shown us how to be more honest in the care of the dying and yet to inspire hope. Love never ends and the power of God's love is not destroyed by death. We see through a mirror darkly but we can safely leave our ultimate future in God's hands. He will not let us down.

☞ *What do we ourselves honestly believe about the nature of life beyond death? What can we say with integrity to those who are dying? Is it right to speak about death as a healing experience?*

Questions for personal written answers or to promote discussion

1. *Think of the different kinds of needs (mental, emotional, physical, spiritual) which come to people at different stages in their lives. What has the Church at any level got to offer to such people? If possible illustrate with specific instances.*

2. *How would you answer a person who says that to be vulnerable is a sign of weakness? Are you conscious of 'wearing a mask' in your own human relationships? Could it sometimes be hurtful to act with total honesty?*

Healing and Stillness

Be still and know that I am God.
Psalm 46:10

The number of people seeking early retirement from the stresses and strains of their working lives seems to increase year by year. Headmasters of schools are now complaining of finding it difficult to fulfil the dual role of being both educators and business managers. Some successful entrepreneurs are trying to make sufficient capital by the time they are fifty – and even earlier – to leave the rat race behind and retire to the highlands of Scotland or some other lonely place. For some it works and they can live fulfilled lives; for others it doesn't and they return to try to discover again their need for a disciplined day in which they have something to do. It is those who have discovered how *to be* as well as *to do* who get the balance right. They can survive either in the solitary place or in the heat of life's endeavours.

The effects of stress upon health and well-being are manifold. Internal struggles affect the chemical metabolism and these can result in stomach and bowel upsets which, if not adequately dealt with, can lead to more serious conditions. Stress, whilst not the only factor in circulatory and heart disease, plays a significant part.

One consultant physician became involved in an experiment some few years ago in which patients were urged to spend time in a retreat centre simply discovering how to relax and find stillness within themselves. We live in a culture where it is commendable to endeavour to rise to the top by virtue of self-effort. (Remember the psychiatrist suggesting that a certain male patient was suffering from a peptic ulcer because he had an over-ambitious wife!)

We make a start on finding an answer to our stress problems when we realise our own need. Because we are lacking satisfaction in our job and perhaps also in our relationships, we feel that we are failing. The answer is that we are and this can be the first step to moving towards a resolution.

Be still

If we actively seek stillness and are willing to get help to find it, we shall succeed. A quiet mind and a willingness to face reality within ourselves will help us to make a start in acquiring a quieter centre at the heart of reality.

Simple relaxation exercise can mark the beginning of the process. Starting with the toes and working upwards through every section of the body – feet, calves, thighs, lower abdomen, chest, neck and head – bring the muscles and nerves first into tension and then, by direct commands, let each part relax. Another way of putting it is to *let go*.

At the same time slow down the breathing process. Breathe deeply and more deliberately from the lower lung area. Avoid at all times shallow breathing in the chest area as this can so easily cause hyperventilation which in turn can cause palpitations so easily mistaken for the symptoms of heart disease.

Accompany these physical actions with quiet remembrance of helpful words like the verse we have taken to trigger this act of devotion.

> Be still and know that I am God.
> In quietness and confidence shall be *my* strength.
> His grace is sufficient for all *my* needs.
> Grow to love silence, but not an empty silence, a godly silence.
> Study to be quiet.
>
> *1 Thessalonians 4:11 (AV)*

> Said the Robin to the Sparrow,
> 'I should really like to know
> Why these anxious human beings
> Rush about and worry so.'
>
> Said the Sparrow to the Robin,
> 'Friend, I think that it must be
> That they have no Heavenly Father
> Such as cares for you and me.'
>
> *Elizabeth Cheney*

If prayer is talking to Jesus, why not stop trying to pray and just talk to him? Why should anyone condemn themselves for the way in which they do or do not pray? There is no special way to pray that wins God's approval. He loves us no matter what we do or how we pray.

from Communicating Love through Prayer
by Rosalind Rinker

One Word spoke the Father
And this Word is his Son.
This Word speaks he ever in eternal silence,
and in silence must it be heard
by the soul.   *St John of the Cross*

Be still and know . . .

There are many ways of knowing. We can amass many facts by reading and listening and study. We can even become an expert upon a particular subject. Factual knowledge is important and useful. We must always try to know what we are talking about. Knowledge, it has been said, is power.

But there is another kind of knowledge which is ultimately much more important. It is the knowledge of awareness – and it comes to us via a very different channel. This particular channel rejects the contemporary world view of success. It is not about occupying powerful positions which give you authority over other people's lives. It is about powerlessness and humility which leads to the ability to influence other people's lives positively and creatively. It is rooted in the acceptance of love and then offering creative love to others. There are two aspects of awareness: awareness of self, and awareness of God – and they go together.

In a famous series of interviews conducted on television by the journalist, John Freeman, perhaps the most significant one of all was with the eminent guru and psychologist, C. G. Jung. At one point Freeman enquired about his faith in God. Did Jung believe? The answer only came after a long and pregnant silence. 'I do not just believe,' said Jung, 'I know.' There was no arrogance in the reply. Just a simple statement of fact. Jung knew!

He also tried to help many people to discover through their own spiritual journeys a greater awareness of themselves. Greater self-knowledge can be devastating, but it can also be wonderfully creative.

In one of our studies we have noted that the phrase 'in Christ' occurs 169 times in the letters of St Paul. What does this mean?

My union with Christ is much more
than an imitation of his virtues
as they are described in the gospel:
it must be a union created in me
by the transforming action of his own Spirit.

And the life which the Spirit
breathes into my spirit,
is Christ Himself mystically present
in my own being and my own person.

from The New Man *by Thomas Merton*

By slowly converting our loneliness into a deep solitude,
we create that precious space where we can discover the
voice telling us about our inner necessity – that is, our
vocation.

from Reaching Out *by Henri Nouwen*

Be still and know that I am God

In the account of Moses meeting with God we read that Moses understood God to say to him: 'I am is sending you.' Later God says to him: 'I
am that I am . . .' The scholars tell us that this means that God is active
and alive, moving out towards his people in the ordinary, everyday
events of life. This sense of the numinous; this greater awareness of
God as being concerned for our own growth and development lies at
the heart of all positive Christian action.

The Bible scholars have identified the message which the early followers
of Jesus presented to the world after the death, resurrection and ascension
of Jesus. It was the *kerygma*, the message about the events which made
up the life of Jesus. It is this message which today will continue to challenge
and stir men and women. To tell the stories of Jesus is to bring God alive
in the ordinary circumstances of life.

David Adam cannot recall where he first heard the following words
but he has given them to us in *The Cry of the Deer*:

> A man with work and no vision is a slave.
> A man with vision and no work is a dreamer.
> A man with vision and work is a prophet.

The vision of Isaiah so wonderfully described in Isaiah Chapter 6
was prior to Isaiah responding to God's call to leadership. Isaiah had to
become acutely aware of the presence of the living God before he
responded to God's call:

> I saw the Lord, high and lifted up.
> Here am I, send me.

That vision so often comes in the stillness. When we are truly quiet
before God we can hear his voice – and his words are life and health
and peace.

> There comes sometimes an interior silence in which the soul
> discovers in itself a new dimension of energy and peace. A
> dimension which the restless life can miss.
>
> *Archbishop Ramsey*

Faith transmutes circumstance,
time, condition and mood
into vitality.
This is why Christ's teaching was
so momentously effective
nineteen centuries ago
and still is so today
among those who truly respond to it.
Then we wake to see with new eyes
and hear with new ears
the beauty and harmony
of God's real world.

Helen Keller

5
Health and Healing Models:
With Suggestions for Church Action

Different people and different professions associated with health and healing approach the subject from a variety of angles. I have identified nine different models. The professionals involved often function through several of the models as do lay people, either as recipients of different forms of treatment or as therapists themselves. Those who function on the basis of one particular model (or a combination of models) would not recognise some of the models I deal with as valid. The criterion I have adopted is that each model has its advocates and practitioners and is, in my view, worthy of careful consideration. Seeing that the Christian faith is concerned with the whole spectrum of life I have asked, in each case, what a truly Christian response might be.

The preventive care model

It is cheaper and better to erect fences at the top of dangerous cliffs than to have a fleet of ambulances always available at the bottom to deal with casualties. In recent years modern medicine and all concerned with health care have come to recognise the value of preventive measures although there are still far more resources devoted to curative practices than to prevention. Diseases of the circulatory system like hypertension, heart attacks and strokes can be prevented by healthier lifestyles. This involves dietary control, reasonably vigorous exercise and not smoking. Excessive intake of alcohol can lead to a variety of illnesses the worst of which is liver failure. Smoking has been clearly demonstrated as having been one of the main causes of lung cancer. Proper diet means more fresh fruit and vegetables, with far less sugar, salt, saturated fat and red meat. Of equal importance is the avoidance of excessive stress and irrational anxiety.

Church action

Where there is inadequate provision of sporting and exercise facilities use Church premises to provide them. This is especially relevant to the older age group including the retired who can organise their own activities given encouragement and adequate facilities. Healthy eating habits can be introduced into our many Church meetings by suitable speakers and we can set a better example in the kind of food we serve at our numerous Church social events. Health education literature might figure more prominently on our bookstalls. The Christian gospel itself is concerned with adequate motivation, and exercise and relaxation classes can be effectively combined with meditation and prayer.

☞ *Do you, the reader, play your part in the above in relation to your own personal lifestyle? Do you encourage your Church to organise healthy, life-enhancing activities?*

The community health model

The corporate health of any community is reflected in the individual health records of its members. Sick communities produce sick people. Those who live in sub-standard housing and live only on social security benefits have a far worse health record than those in the middle and professional classes. Sir Douglas Black chaired a committee set up by the government many years ago to enquire into the reasons why this was so. The answers the committee came up with in *The Black Report* were not politically acceptable and so were quietly shelved. They were to the effect that changes were needed in housing policy, welfare benefits, social provision and education including school meals. All were changes which involved greater expenditure from the public purse.

Community development methods would enable people to help themselves but resources are required to spark the action. Primary health care could lay more emphasis on preventive care by organising, through GP practices and health centres, health education courses such as the 'Well Woman' and now 'Well Man' clinics. A community development worker attached to each practice and health centre could eventually produce results which would entirely justify the expenditure involved. This is already happening in more primitive societies where the village health workers are showing that their presence in many small communities is a far better use of resources than a high-tech hospital in a centre many miles away from most potential patients. (Of course ideally we need both.) Pre-school play groups and Pensioners' Clubs are fruitful fields of activity for a community development health worker thus relating to both extremes of the age range.

Church action

Set up working parties to enquire into local health care policies and seek to influence them by encouraging Church members to serve on Health Authorities and Community Health Councils. Encourage Church members to take a greater interest in their own GP practice and health centre and be willing to serve on the support groups many practices are establishing. Arrange courses as part of the Church programme dealing with health and healing issues. Bring such issues into worship especially on Hospital Sunday and around St Luke's day.

☞ *Do I tend to restrict Christian activity to what I deem to be truly spiritual, such as praying for the sick and special healing services? Do I personally need to live on a larger map and develop wider horizons?*

The scientific medical model

In the main this is the province of doctors but we, the consumers, are often at the receiving end of medical care based on this premise. Basically it is that every illness has a cause which must be traced by a variety of investigative methods and when located in a particular organ given the appropriate treatment. Hence the variety of specialists who concentrate on their own narrow field. This model has been wonderfully successful in treating and indeed conquering many illnesses. But it has its weaknesses. Some illnesses are difficult to diagnose and would seem to relate to the kind of person the patient is rather than being precisely located in one particular area. Even if diagnosis is possible, the real cause may well lie outside the patient in family and/or community pressures. Thus health is described in functional terms as the absence of illness and seems to rely upon drugs more than upon education and greater self-awareness. It also tends to create a 'pill for every ill' syndrome in patients.

Church action

Encourage Church members to make the best use of the doctor-patient relationship by seeking to be involved in a better understanding of their own health needs. Ask for possible alternatives to drug treatments and always enquire about their side-effects. Draw Church members' attention to the next model which many doctors are coming to appreciate more and more.

☞ *What kind of relationship do I have with my own doctor? Do I feel that I can speak to him openly and honestly? If he or she suggests that we leave it to them as they are professionally trained, ought we to consider making a move to a new doctor?*

The holistic health model

There is in existence a British Holistic Medical Association with its first Chairman being Dr Patrick Pietroni. The emphasis here is much more on treating the patient as a person than as a sick patient. One of the maxims of the Association is that 'we treat the person not just the illness'. Much illness is due to a state of imbalance; a condition of internal disharmony which has chemical results. Guilt or anxiety (popularly known as worry) may be a factor and certainly relationships with other people are likely to be involved. The doctor who works with this model will need to be more than a medical technician; he or she must have a considerable degree of self-awareness which will enable a relationship of trust to be established with the patient. Many holistic medical practitioners find it perfectly reasonable to work in co-operation with complementary therapists and others have themselves become trained in disciplines such as homeopathy, acupuncture and yoga. There is also a greater willingness to co-operate with priests, ministers and lay counsellors. The spiritual component of the person in need is taken very seriously and self-help groups are often sponsored by doctors working in this way.

Church action

Find out which doctors in your area are sympathetic to this approach and may be linked with the BHMA. Invite them to speak at Church meetings and offer co-operation in accommodating self-help groups. Do the same with reputable complementary therapists. Consider the provision of a trained counselling service along the lines of the next model to be considered. This service could be at two levels. First, that of sympathetic and understanding listeners. Training courses in the art of listening are provided in various parts of the country by the Acorn Christian Healing Trust. As already indicted, the Revd Anne Long has initiated these courses and has written a book entitled Listening *(published by Daybreak). The second level can be that of trained counsellors based on the insights of psychotherapy. Once these are established local medical practices can be informed. There is growing evidence of the willingness of some doctors to make use of these facilities. See also the book by Patrick Pietroni* Holistic Living *(published by Dent Paperbacks).*

☞ *Do I feel that I can talk to my own doctor along these lines? Without giving the impression that you want to treat yourself ask to be taken seriously in your endeavours to gain greater self-awareness and so to adjust your lifestyle as to make a greater contribution towards your own health and well-being. Talk to other like-minded people and perhaps form a self-help group.*

The pastoral counselling model

This relates to the previous model but is also a model in its own right. Many areas have highly developed centres and there are national Church-based organisations such as the Westminster Pastoral Foundation. The aim is to help clients to discover greater personal awareness which leads to personality growth and developing maturity. As this happens the counsellor gradually withdraws from the scene. One of the consequences may be an improvement in physical health as the person in need progresses towards a more balanced life-style in which he or she discovers a growing sense of satisfaction.

A more recent development is *Prayer Counselling.* This involves two people meeting with the client and is concerned to help the client to become aware of hidden memories which may be contributing to their condition. This discovery may then be offered to God in prayer or in a celebration of Holy Communion. There is always a danger that inexperienced counsellors may feel that a direct spiritual approach must always work. In fact it doesn't and lack of experience and training can give people false hopes which, when unfulfilled, mean that people get worse rather than better. In appropriate circumstances, however, and with skilled handling, the introduction of the spiritual dimension can be effective.

Church action

Provide trained befrienders and counsellors wherever this is possible. If it isn't, become aware of where such help can be found. Relate *(formerly Marriage Guidance) can always be relied upon for high levels of training but, although having distinctive Christian origins, now functions within a secular and multi-faith context. Those Christians and Church members who are* Relate *counsellors may be willing to help service the local Churches' pastoral care organisations. This is done by giving simple training to all pastoral visitors to help them to make better use of the relationships they have with those who have been put under their care. My own little book* Healing through Caring *(published by Arthur James) was written specifically for this purpose.*

Prayer Counselling could be investigated and where and when it seems right, utilised in the service of needy people. Prayer, however, is a part of all Christian caring. Prayer Counselling is a distinctive method, and is a discipline in its own right.

☞ *Do I feel myself adequately equipped to help others in need? Should I seek further training? How can I encourage my Church to realise that pastoral care is more than just visiting people and say, delivering a monthly magazine. Encourage your Church to investigate how a pastoral care training course can be arranged.*

The direct ministry model

This model embraces three combined approaches. First of all, prayer either within worship or through separate prayer groups. Individuals are prayed for; time being spent carefully thinking and praying for each individual person. We are all linked together, 'bound up in the bundle of life' as the Bible says and we participate at a deep level in what Jung called 'the collective unconscious'. By linking the person at the heart of our prayers with the living God we are establishing channels of grace. Another way of expressing what is happening is that we are linking a person's needs with God's ongoing creative powers. This is then backed up by the laying on of hands often within a special healing service. In some cases this is supplemented by anointing with oil.

All these ways of ministering to people require careful preparation. God's grace visits individuals in different ways with different consequences. Obviously the main desire in many people's minds, when they are seriously ill, is to recover from that illness and be restored to health. Our desires are well understood by our Heavenly Father. Our approach to God for ourselves and for others should not be restricted to our own well-understood desires. Sometimes God responds in different ways which in his good time we shall understand. Certainly no wild and exaggerated promises should be made. When recognisable improvement takes place we should give thanks to God but not necessarily blazon it abroad. Pastoral sensitivity requires that we always remember those who desire similar improvement but for whom this does not happen. Teaching about all aspects of the direct ministry model needs to be a regular feature in the local Church's Christian education programmes.

Church action

As indicated above, careful preparation of the local Church's activity is needed to help people to see that the healing ministry is an essential part of the Church's regular witness. Healing prayer groups and healing services with the laying-on of hands and anointing should only be started when the whole matter has been fully discussed in the appropriate Church courts. A few individuals should not be allowed either to impose their wishes upon a congregation or, because they object, prohibit such activities from taking place. Every effort should be made to ensure that healing ministry is never divisive.

☞ *Have I received benefit from healing prayer groups, the laying-on of hands and/or anointing? Do I have confidence in such practices if I am without direct personal experience? Does my Church need to be challenged about the possibilities of developing such activities as a regular feature in its ministry?*

The deliverance model

This particular model is perhaps the most controversial of all and because of this is dealt with at greater length in the next chapter in this study guide. However, it is a model which is widely used in some Church circles and there is an extremely reputable organisation entitled The Churches' Fellowship for Psychic and Spiritual Studies which makes a careful and critical study of psychic phenomena.

This model majors on the deliverance from the power of evil spirits where these have been identified in personal, family and home situations. This deliverance is offered in the name of Jesus and by the power of the Holy Spirit. The position taken by the present writer is that many of the cases which some Christians attribute to the presence of evil spirits are actually personality disorders which are best dealt with by a combination of psychiatric and pastoral care. The background of those concerned always needs to be carefully investigated by both medical and psychological professionals. Sometimes there can be a physical and chemical explanation for certain forms of bizarre behaviour. However, a purely rational explanation for all forms of unusual behaviour is not easily found. There is also the point that you do not have to have a considered belief in the objective reality of evil, demonic spirits in order to relate to those who believe that they are possessed. You can meet them at the level of their own understanding and meet the challenge they present by invoking the power of Jesus and possibly celebrating the Holy Eucharist. It should be noted, however, that where there is a great deal of discussion about demonic invasion it is in these communities that such phenomena more readily appear.

Church action

Study the report entitled Deliverance *(SPCK) edited by Michael Perry who is Archdeacon of Durham and also Editor of the Journal,* Christian Parapsychologist. Deliverance *is the result of several years work by a group which numbered among its members those with medical, psychiatric and pastoral expertise. If individual Church members get involved with those who believe themselves to be possessed they should listen carefully, endeavour to keep calm and pray inwardly. It is not wise to treat such people with open scepticism. Whatever the reality of their situation they are in real need. The Church of England has advisors on the paranormal and they are usually prepared to assist those of other Churches. Especially note the point made above about ministering to people at the level of their own understanding. For instance, if a person believes that a curse has been placed upon them they will not easily be reasoned out of such a belief. Direct action to break the 'curse' in the name of Jesus is likely to have a more positive result.*

☞ *What is my own understanding of demonic possession? Have I thought about how I would act if faced with a person who believes themselves to be possessed? Can a belief in being possessed by an evil spirit sometimes be a way of avoiding personal responsibility?*

The miracle model

The miracle model is an attractive one. Whenever people are healed and prayer and direct ministry are involved, this is most encouraging to faith and it is often the case that the incident is talked (and written) about a great deal. Francis MacNutt, the Roman Catholic charismatic leader who was once a priest but who is now married and laicised, says that 75 per cent of those with physical and emotional ailments, when they are prayed for, experience healing. He does, however, qualify this by adding that usually people are not completely healed by prayer but they are helped and improved. A consultant obstetrician, who is also a minister in the Free Church of Scotland, has conducted an exhaustive examination of many cases of reported healing miracles. He does himself take an overt evangelical position and is sympathetic to charismatic renewal. His final conclusions are restrained and sober. They are that when all other explanations (psychosomatic illness, natural remission, adjunct medical therapy, etc.) have been eliminated, there remain some cures for which modern medicine has no explanation. Nevertheless only a small percentage of those who seek physical healing from God, obtain it. (See *Healing Miracles* by Rex Gardner, published by Darton, Longman and Todd.)

Church action

Miracles inspire hope and they do occur from time to time. We should encourage the faithful to expect that God will work in human lives because that is what the doctrine of grace is all about – God in action working positively for human good. But we must beware of the kind of approach to God which seems to insist that he must respond in exactly the way we desire. Healing and cure do not always go together and this is not just double-talk as some would insist. Expectations of inexplicable happenings must always be tempered by pastoral concern for those who long for such miracles to happen but do not experience them. We must also beware of being taken over by the 'miracle syndrome', so that we fail to see God at work in what may seem to be ordinary healing activity such as that which comes via medicine, surgery, psychotherapy and simple human love and care.

☞ *Have I any direct, personal experience of healing events I would describe as miracles? In praying with and for people can I strike the right balance between hope and realism? Is it possible to trust God where you cannot always trace God and if so may the main motivation for my prayers be that I – and those for whom I pray – may rest in God's eternal changlessness and never-failing love?*

The healing gift model

Certain individuals do seem to have a healing gift which enables them to be of great help to other people in a variety of needs and conditions. Many are Christians who believe that their gift has been given in accordance with the statement made in 1 Corinthians 12:9. Others are not committed Christians but are imbued with a kind of healing energy which they are able to share with others and thus give a 'kick-start' to that person's own self-healing powers.

The test is always 'by their fruits you shall know them'. If they are humble and do not seek excessive financial gain from their healing activities then their ministry can be accepted gratefully. Most such healers function through their hands and seek to establish rapport with those they are seeking to help.

Church action

Those who practise the use of such a gift from within the fellowship of the local Church should be encouraged to offer their gift to God and use it quietly and with restraint as a part of the Church's overall healing ministry. Attempts to exalt such people should be avoided as this will give rise to a belief on the part of some that they have magic powers. Within healing services those with a healing gift should be used as part of the team that has been trained and prepared to play their part. The Lord only is the healer and we can all co-operate in establishing those channels through which he works.

☞ *Could it be that I myself have an undiscovered healing gift? Might its source and origin be in the way we have become aware that we are loved by God and thus able to love others? Is the gift of love the greatest healing gift of all?*

Questions for personal written answers or to promote discussion

1. *Go through each of the models mentioned and decide upon those of which you totally approve and those about which you have reservations. If within a group, discuss why this is and see if further enlightenment comes from your sharing your insights with one another. If working independently, note those of which you approve and then set out your reasons for having reservations about the others.*

2. *Have you any experience of those who work with the medical model being willing to share in the care of patients with those who practise the direct ministry model? Set out the issues you feel may arise when professionally trained doctors and nurses and other therapists are invited to work alongside those who are working on what might be described as a spiritual model. If in a group, share both experiences and ideas and decide if any of the models are totally or partially unacceptable.*

3. *Is your Church offering any guidance to its members about their being involved (either as therapists or recipients) in the various models outlined in this chapter? Consider in what ways you could work to bring about some consideration of all the issues involved. If working as an individual, write an article for your Church magazine setting out your proposals. If within a group, decide together upon what should be included in such an article.*

Creation and Creativity

Give thanks for creation

Reflect on how you came into being. Give thanks for your parents but then wander back down your family tree. You may not be able to get very far but you are part of a line that goes back and back into the mists of time. The mind finds endless time hard to grasp but for us there was a beginning . . .

In the beginning – God

At the very beginning of all things
God made the universe we know.

The earth lay empty and dead,
darkness blacked out the deep seas,
great winds lashed the water.

God spoke –
'Let there be light'
and the world was filled with light.

From the beginning – Jesus

The word became human
and lived a human life like ours.

We saw his splendour,
love's splendour, real splendour.

Nobody has ever seen God himself;
the beloved Son,
who knows his Father's secret thoughts,
has made him plain.

from New World *by Alan T. Dale*

Reflect on the creative life of Jesus

Remember:

> We are God's handiwork, created in Christ Jesus for the
> life of good deeds which God designed for us.
> *Ephesians 2:10*

Formal religion can become so trivial and even meaningless. We can get caught up in Church politics and neglect the heart of the matter. The remedy – get back to Jesus. Think about him. What he said. What he did. How he cared. Most of all how he loved. Think about the creative death of Jesus which was the focal point of his God-disclosure.

> He died that we might be forgiven,
> He died to make us good.
> That we might go at last to heaven,
> Saved by his precious blood
> *Cecil Frances Alexander*

God's creative energies are so beautifully expressed in this poem:

> Love alone is supreme
> This I believe
> And out of formless chaos did conceive
> Purpose and design.
> So came to birth
> Fondly wrapped in loveliness
> This earth.
>
> God's very self, Jesus the anointed one,
> Perfect revealer of God's face, Mary's son,
> Living in time and in recorded history
> Dying a felon's death.
> The mystery!
>
> That life itself should die to rise again;
> Wholeness made whole in majesty to reign.
> That through the light that is in Christ alone
> The whole truth about us all is known.
>
> The Advocate is with us when we meet
> We are the body of Christ, heart, hands and feet;
> Forgiven, redeemed, together bound
> Into a mystic fellowship profound,

Yet still myself, though I will come to be
Remade, O Christ, and wholly one with thee.
This I believe, Amen, I seek to say,
Help thou mine unbelief, Thou living way.

The Creed of Liberty *by Phoebe Willetts*

Link God's love revealed in Jesus and kept alive by the Holy Spirit with your own pursuit of wholeness

Read Psalm 1 slowly and deliberately and then concentrate on verses 2 and 3:

His delight is in the law of the Lord;
it is his meditation day and night.
He is like a tree
planted beside water channels;
it yields its fruit in season
and its foliage never fades.

Remember it is the gardener who plants, thus it is God who takes the initiative. Our response is to constantly put ourselves in those places where growth and development are possible. See the roots of your life thrust deep into the life and love of God.

See the fruit bearing branches with their harvest of golden, ripe fruits. You are one of them. God says to you: 'Go and bear fruit'.

Be aware that even in the dry seasons the tree, because of its location by the water channels, continues to bear fruit. Nevertheless, be ready for the dry seasons.

When dark nights come to me,
Let your love flow through me.
When the desert overwhelms me,
May supporting grace deliver me.

The Apostle Paul sometimes sank low,
His 'flesh-thorn' caused him sorrow.
You gave him strength in weakness – so –
Grant us a bright tomorrow.

Your promises are firm and true,
Enabling growth in times of stress.
We would grow tall and strong in you,
Though painful be the process.

To bear much fruit is our desire,
Grant us the joy of reaping;
Renewed by your refining fire,
To celebrate with joy and singing.

from Seven Whole Days

Now remember that you are to share in God's creativity

We all tend to undervalue our own creative abilities. A woman who had attended a banner-making course was soon involved herself. She looked up to a bystander and said, 'I didn't realise that I had it in me.'

Those who attend courses run by the Creative Arts Network are slow at first to get involved. Then suddenly in one art form or another they discover their hitherto undiscovered talent. Once they offer it to God it increases both in quality and in application.

You are the God of every human being
and, too dazzling to be looked at,
you let yourself be seen as in a mirror,
shining on the face of Christ.
We are eager
to glimpse a reflection of your presence
in the obscurity of persons and events –
so open in us the gates of transparency
of
heart.
In that portion of solitude
which is the lot of everyone,
come and refresh
the dry and thirsty ground of our body,
and our spirit.
Come and place a spring of living water
in the lifeless regions of our being.
Come and bathe us in your confidence
to make even our inner deserts
burst into flower.

Brother Roger of Taizé

God be in my head, and in my understanding;

God be in mine eyes and in my looking;

God be in my mouth and in my speaking;

God be in my heart, and in my thinking;

God be at mine end, and at my departing.

The Book of Hours, 1514

O Lord, may I be a window through which those who look into me may see Jesus. So shall I share in your ongoing creation.

The entire theme of this meditation is expressed in a hymn I once wrote for a Harvest Festival:

Sharing in Creation

Father, we thank you,
For your creation.
Blessings abound,
Wherever we gaze.
Bright greens of nature,
Blend all together,
Patterns of hedgerows,
Ever amaze.

O what a joy,
To share in creation,
With fruits of our minds,
And work of our hands.
You gave the gifts,
Which we can develop.
May what we offer,
Serve many lands.

Here in our own midst,
People are needy,
Some have no homes;
Find life very tough.
Show us how sharing,
What you have given,
Saves them from feeling,
Life is too rough.

Jesus, our Saviour,
Living among us,
Our new creator,
Show us the way.
Shape us as models,
Of your new era.
Inspire our thinking,
All that we say.

So shall your Kingdom,
Ever increasing,
Use all the gifts,
We offer today.
This is the hope,
Inspiring our worship,
As at your feet,
Our talents we lay.

Can be sung to the tune Bunessan

6
Demons and the Demonic

In 1976 in Barnsley a woman was murdered by her husband after an all-night exorcism had taken place during which a group of Pentecostal Christians claimed to have exorcised many demons from him but had failed to exorcise the demon of murder. In 1993 a woman was killed in an Australian country town when her larynx was crushed during an exorcism. (As reported in *Sent to Heal* by Harold Taylor, published by the Order of St Luke.)

Both these sensational incidents gave rise to careful investigations by the major Christian Churches, and certainly, following on from the 'Barnsley' incident, they reviewed their policy and practice on exorcism at national level.

As I was involved at that time with The Methodist Church's Committee on Healing I recall that this committee was requested by the Methodist Conference to take counsel with the Faith and Order Committee and produce a report and recommendations. This we did and the consequent Statement began by setting out three different positions which are all held, genuinely and sincerely, by Christian believers, about the existence of demons.

1. *Demons do exist as an objective reality and can possess individuals. The power to exorcise these demons has been given to the Church as one way in which Christ's ministry is expressed in the world.*

2. *Demons do not exist as objective realities but people who believe themselves to be possessed may be exorcised. In such cases it is the psychological reality of the experience of possession which is being dealt with.*

3. *A belief in demons is explicable on the basis of psychological and sociological research. Exorcism is not therefore appropriate, since what is being dealt with is false belief. The proper response is skilled pastoral care linked with the normal ministry of word and sacraments.*

There then followed a series of Guidelines which indicated a cautious approach in which there should be full consultation with persons suitably qualified in medicine, psychology and the social services. No one (minister or lay person) should act independently and there should always be consultation with colleagues and senior ministers. Priority should always be given to pastoral care but if any service was held to exorcise or seek to deliver any individual from what appeared to be demonic activity the whole exercise should be carefully considered and the service conducted within a quiet and restrained atmosphere.

The Bible background

Demons are a feature of all primitive religions and this was certainly so in the early religion of Israel. However, there slowly emerged a belief in the omnipresence and omnipotence of Yahweh, bringer of good and evil. The powers of evil existed but their authority was circumscribed (see Psalm 89:10 and Isaiah 51:9).

However, evil was a force to be reckoned with and there had to be some kind of explanation for its reality which did not compromise the ultimate power and authority of Yahweh. Satan (the adversary) first emerged without a capital 'S'. See 1 Samuel 29:4 where the Philistines distrust David and send him back in case 'in the battle he became an *adversary* (Hebrew: satan) to us'.

In the Book of Job (Chapters 1 and 2) 'the Satan' becomes a title for an adversary and tester of human beings, but he always works under God's orders and within God's limits (Job 1:12 and 2:6). In Zechariah 3:1 Satan has become the false accuser of Joshua but he is rebuked by God. In 1 Chronicles 21:1 Satan is the name given to the adversary of God and men (but compare 2 Samuel 24:1).

The inter-testamental period saw different understandings of the role of Satan but eventually he became perceived as the 'chief demon' leading his army of demons over against God's army of angels. Theories eventually developed relating Satan to the fall and identifying him with the serpent in Genesis 3. So Satan is God's arch-enemy but the New Testament also makes clear that he has been defeated. With the incarnation of Jesus the Kingdom of God has been inaugurated and victory is assured. The Temptation and the wilderness experiences demonstrated who was Master! (Luke 4:2; Mark 1:13; and Matthew

4:1). Jesus later prayed for his disciples that they should not come under Satan's sway (Luke 22:31), and especially for Peter, that, when he had recovered from his failure, he would give strength to his companions (Luke 22:32).

Jesus lived and ministered within a culture which accepted demons as valid explanations for phenomena which, today, would largely be accounted for by medical and psychiatric diagnoses. The boy whose story is told in Mark 9:14-29 was evidently suffering from epilepsy. The Gadarene demoniac of Mark 5:2-7 would now be recognised as suffering from a manic-depressive psychosis. The cultural climate, however, whilst important, is of less significance than the mighty acts which Jesus performed. The Kingdom which he inaugurated and proclaimed was demonstrated by his deeds and the power of Jesus over demons of any kind is evident from Matthew 12:28: 'But if it is by the Spirit of God that I cast out demons, then the Kingdom of God has come upon you.'

Charles Wesley expressed this so magnificently when he wrote:

> Jesus – the name high over all,
> In hell or earth or sky!
> Angels and men before it fall,
> And devils fear and fly.

It should further be noted that there are many healing acts of Jesus recorded in the New Testament which do not describe the disease or illness as being due to the work of Satan or demons: the nobleman's son (John 4:52); Peter's mother-in-law (Mark 1:30); the paralytic (Mark 2:3) and many more. These gracious acts were the response of his love and compassion to human need. It was often through his touch and the assurance of forgiveness that healing came.

There is however a difference of emphasis between biblical scholars. Dr J. Keir Howard, writing in the *Expository Times* of January 1985, expressed a belief that:

> These disordered biochemical mechanisms which lie behind most forms of mental illness are gradually being elucidated, and such conditions should be seen as essentially no different from other manifestations of deranged bio-chemistry such as diabetes mellitus or an over-active thyroid gland.

However Dr Graham Twelvetree and Professor J. D. G. Dunn, writing in *Churchman* in 1980, whilst agreeing that by no means all illnesses were attributed to demons and demon possession, saw the concept of demon possession as being reserved for

> conditions where the individual seemed to be totally in the grip of an evil power (using his vocal chords, Mark 1:24, 5:7, 9; Acts 16:16; convulsing him, Mark 1:26, 9:20-22, 26; superhuman strength, Mark 5:3-4; Acts 19:16).

Dr Twelvetree, writing on his own account in *Christ Triumphant,* is convinced that:

> Jesus was certainly an exorcist, like others of his time, but we cannot claim that exorcism was the key to his ministry; simply with Matthew 12:28 and Luke 11:20 in mind that exorcism was at least one of the important functions or aspects of his ministry.
>
> *from* Deliverance *edited by Michael Perry*

We can therefore see that exorcisms were not a major factor in the public ministry of Jesus but that Jesus did practise exorcism in certain specific cases when he thought such a ministry was appropriate. In his letters Paul does not say a great deal about demon possession but he does refer to 'the spiritual hosts of wickedness in high places' (Ephesians 6:12) and Satan is identified in 1 Corinthians 5:5 and 1 Thessalonians 2:18, but these could easily be his descriptive way of referring to the power of evil (sin) which he so eloquently describes in Romans 6. The early Church continued to exorcise but it does seem to have happened less and less frequently and in some parts of the Church hardly at all.

☞ *What do you think of this quote from* The Screwtape Letters *by C. S. Lewis?: 'There are two equal and opposite errors into which our race can fall about devils; one is to disbelieve in their existence, the other is to feel an excessive and unhealthy interest in them. They themselves are equally pleased by both errors and hail a materialist or a magician with the same delight.'*

Exorcism and deliverance ministries within the Churches today

It should first be noted that those Churches which practise exorcism and deliverance ministries generally distinguish between the two. In the book already referred to, namely *Deliverance,* this distinction is described in the following terms:

> Exorcism is a specific act of binding and releasing, performed on a person who is believed to be possessed by a non-human malevolent spirit . . . Deliverance is about freeing people from the bondage of Satan. It may occasionally involve exorcism but generally it does not. It is important to reserve exorcism for those few cases where it is appropriate and necessary.

The Roman Catholic Church recognises this distinction by differentiating between Solemn and Private (or Simple) Exorcism. The former can only be performed by a consecrated minister (priest) acting under the appropriate authority. Private exorcisms may be performed by priests and laity and no permission is required. Francis MacNutt, a leading Roman Catholic charismatic (once a priest but now laicised), says that possession is rare but people being *demonised* is a more frequent occurrence. He thus distinguishes between people being taken over by a malevolent and evil spirit, and people being affected by the results of folly, unbelief or sin.

Father Sean Conaty in an article in *The Christian Parapsychologist* (March 1988) suggests that Francis MacNutt is actually putting into practice Catholic pastoral and moral teaching. The form of deliverance ministry he exercises relates to Simple Exorcism. He believes that most Roman Catholic priests today think of exorcism only in terms of Solemn and Public Exorcism for which the Bishop's permission is needed. Because of this they deprive themselves of a pastoral means of grace.

In the Church of England the practice of exorcism is regularised through the Diocesan Bishops, who should each appoint an *Adviser.* In most cases a team is established to deal with such matters and this often includes a psychiatrist and doctor as well as a priest or priests. The task of such a group is to advise the priest in pastoral charge how he might tackle a particular situation and what kind of help he might seek. In practice other denominations also make use of this facility. In 1972 the Exeter Commission stated:

There are many men and women so under the grip of the power of evil that they need the help of the Christian Church in delivering them from it. When this ministry is carried out the following factors should be borne in mind:

1. It should be done in collaboration with the resources of medicine.
2. It should be done in the context of prayer and sacrament.
3. It should be done with the minimum of publicity.
4. It should be done by experienced persons authorised by the Diocesan Bishop.
5. It should be followed up by continuous pastoral care.

The Church of Scotland takes a totally different line in its official pronouncements and states:

> Such a ceremonial as exorcism does more harm than good by its existence within the practice of the Church. We believe that it effects nothing which cannot be accomplished by the expeditious use of medical and pastoral skills . . . there is no place in the Reformed Scottish Church for such a rite to be devised . . . Any person encountering a case of alleged possession should refer it to a physician.
>
> *report of a working party on parapsychology, May 1976*

The position taken by the Methodist Church is set out in the early paragraphs of this chapter. In practice it closely resembles the suggestions for pastoral practice laid down by the Exeter Commission of the Church of England.

☞ *Have you come into contact with any individuals where demon possession is thought to have been the cause of distress? Most working priests and ministers will only meet up with three or four such cases in a lifetime's ministry. In the light of the above what kind of action would you take if such a situation did arise.*

Charismatic renewal movements and the house Churches

In an article entitled 'Evangelicals and the Deliverance Ministry' in *The Christian Parapsychologist* (March 1988), John Allan refers to the variety of views and practices about deliverance ministries within the evangelical Churches. An evangelical himself, he writes:

> There is no one agreed theology of the demonic, no common approach to deliverance ministry shared by evangelicals of different strains.

For many years evangelicals, tracing their original inspiration back to the Reformation discovery of justification by faith, suspected would-be exorcists as vulgar magicians. Many followed the dispensationalist theory, believing that the healing miracles of Jesus of every kind were intended to demonstrate his uniqueness and Messiahship. Once this was securely established the *dispensation* was over and we should not now expect miracles of the New Testament pattern.

Charismatic renewal has, however, brought about many changes within the conservative evangelical fold, not least in the changed attitude towards Roman Catholics, and there have been some notable changes of mind about deliverance ministries as exercised by charismatics, notably the growth of an accord between the charismatic leader, Michael Harper and the leading conservative evangelical, John Stott.

It is the growth of the charismatic movement within the mainline Churches and the increase in the number of house Churches (with their varying emphases) which have brought deliverance ministries into prominence. People within our Churches are being affected by them, sometimes apparently positively but equally sometimes negatively and occasionally quite disastrously. The events which accompany such ministries, such as convulsions, people falling limp to the ground sometimes described as being slain in the Spirit, are disturbing to many. Now we have the arrival of the Toronto Blessing with its even more strange consequences of ecstatic noises such as barking like dogs. The question which hangs over all these varied phenomena is surely: *Do they produce that most important of all gifts of the Spirit, the gift of love?*

John Wimber has powerfully influenced the charismatic scene in this country and he believes in *demonisation* rather than *possession* (i.e. people being adversely affected by demonic activity but not completely taken over). Wimber quotes extensively from *The Screwtape Letters* by C. S. Lewis, although I seriously doubt whether their basic theological positions are similar. The C. S. Lewis classic is a persuasive and delightful allegory of the ways in which evil flourishes both in society and in the human heart. Wimber sees Satan or the Devil as an actual malevolent being, rather than the symbol of the powers of evil and darkness which are so evident in our modern world. He does not believe in overall possession but in widespread demonisation on a kind of sliding scale. (See his book *Power Healing* written with Kevin Springer and published by Hodder in 1986.) In this book he details a list of symptoms for which he believes deliverance ministries are appropriate. These include drug or alcohol addiction, masturbation, homosexuality, eating disorders, self-hatred, bitterness, etc. True, he does enter a caveat when he states that 'the presence of one or more of these symptoms indicates the possibility though not the necessity that a person is demonised'. In spite of his caveat many pastors and psychiatrists would regard many of the conditions he describes as being due to personality disorders and inadequacies which can be treated by acceptance, understanding, counselling, psychotherapy and group therapy. Most would also regard homosexuality as being related to genetic disposition. The idea that those of homosexual orientation have been demonised is totally unacceptable.

☞ *Charismatic renewal has influenced the whole Church through its music, its liberation of worship and its encouragement of personal testimony. Do you feel personally the benefits of these developments? In some Churches however it appears to have been divisive and there are many reports of casualties who have required much loving and skilled pastoral care to hold them within Christ's flock. Have you experienced a balanced approach to charismatic renewal or have you been put off by extremists? How can we harness the positive aspects and deal with the unacceptable?*

The contribution of the behavioural sciences

In general, psychiatrists regard people who believe that they are possessed by demons to be deluded. They are suffering from one or other form of mental illness which, they hold, can in many cases be diagnosed and treated. The majority would support the following:

1. *Psychiatrists would look first for a combination of physical, mental and social factors. The physical basis may be hormonal imbalance. The mental factor may be a guilt complex having its origin in immature religious concepts. The social factor may be the environment in which they have been brought up and the pressures they have been under since their earliest days. Get the hormonal imbalance right and you are on the way to a cure. Psychotherapy, giving greater self-awareness, may add a further dimension to the 'deliverance' of the persons concerned.*

2. *Schizophrenia is now widely regarded as having a physical basis. It can be controlled and directed by the use of well-known drugs. Exorcism or deliverance ministries are totally irrelevant to people suffering from schizophrenia.*

3. *Drug addiction (including alcohol) can block the neural mechanisms with bizarre consequences, including the delusion that one is possessed. A combination of medical, psychiatric and spiritual care is called for here and it is often a long up-hill road to sanity and self-control.*

4. *Neurotic illness, of which the best known is irrational anxiety, can be greatly exacerbated by deliverance enthusiasts. Repressed parts of the personality which have been under control may be released in a highly charged emotional atmosphere. The later consequences may be disastrous.*

5. *Some people are highly suggestible. In an environment where daily life is full of anxiety and lacking in motivation, a strong individual or group personality can impress such people with ideas on demon possession, and they will then be easily convinced that they themselves are possessed and in need of deliverance or exorcism.*

Bearing in mind all these factors it is essential that renewal movements within the main-line Churches and equally within the house and community Churches, develop mature and understanding leadership. The re-emphasis upon the work of the Holy Spirit is to be welcomed but enthusiasm alone is not sufficient. The observable facts are that where there is much talk about demons and demonisation this creates the atmosphere in which increasing numbers of people believe that they are possessed. Such happenings guarantee attention and can be a subtle means of avoiding personal responsibility.

Alternative Christian attitudes

These have already been given within this chapter but for convenience they can now be summarised as follows:

1. *Demons are not objective realities and possession by them is impossible. This is the official line taken by the Church of Scotland but I suspect that many individual Church of Scotland ministers and members do not accept it.*

2. *The second is the exact opposite and has been expressed by John Wimber in the book* Power Healing *already referred to. The Devil (Satan) is an objective reality (although not equal with God). Others will take a similar line with some variations. The consequence of this belief is that deliverance ministry and exorcism are regular features of Christian ministry. Although the distinction has been made between a deliverance and an exorcism, in practice there is little difference between them. For some reason deliverance is a more acceptable word than exorcism.*

3. *The third position is that taken by the main-line denominations through their official statements, although within the parameters of those statements there is a wide variety of emphases. The style of ministry suggested does not depend upon an actual belief in the separate, objective reality of demons, although many individuals will take this view.*

Alec Vidler puts it this way in one of his Windsor sermons:

> You do not have to bother whether the Devil is best described as a person or a supernatural agency – so long as you take him seriously. What you have to do is not to define him but renounce him.

I would want to endorse this but I am also strongly attracted to the position held by Father Christopher Bryant and expressed in his book *Journey to the Centre* (Darton, Longman and Todd, 1987):

> Modern psychologists speak of autonomous complexes, little bundles of psychic energy, which operate independently of our conscious will; they act like sub-personalities, and we may have a truer understanding of them if we think of them as spirits at work within us rather than abstractions.

The over-riding consideration in every case of human need, whatever way we understand the cause of the problem, is the best possible kind of care we can give or arrange. All who subscribe to this third position would agree that the majority of those cases presented as either demonisation or possession are best dealt with by a combination of medical, psychiatric and spiritual care, this latter backed by prayer, the invitation to confession and the assurance of forgiveness. This may also include anointing and/or the laying-on of hands preferably within the context of the Eucharist.

However, this does leave room for a formal ministry of deliverance after the due processes of consultation have been gone through. This should be a quiet and reverent ceremony with the person concerned being in as relaxed a state as is possible. In getting on for half a century of pastoral ministry I have only been asked for one such service where an individual was concerned. Others have related to houses and particular rooms and after due consideration I have been pleased to help and there have always been positive results. (See next section.)

The primary task of any Christian community is not to cast out but to shed abroad the love of Jesus into the hearts and lives of people and communities. As we exalt him so the powers of darkness will fear and flee, whatever their origin or nature.

☞ *Reflect upon the different positions held by individuals and groups within the fellowship of the ecumenical Church. Decide upon what you feel to be your own position. Have you discussed this with Christian friends say from within your own Church? If you feel nervous about this, think of what the consequences of total avoidance of these matters might be.*

Places not persons

As indicated already most pastors and priests who have experienced requests for help in connection with unusual phenomena which have been attributed to the work of evil spirits have found that these requests related more often to buildings, rooms or places than to individual human beings. The first category we may describe as *poltergeist phenomena.* The actual happenings differ widely but the most common are noises of different kinds, articles being moved, water dripping, doors opening and closing of their own accord, strange smells and cold spots.

The possibility of trickery or deceit should always be examined. This is especially likely where the occupant(s) of the premises where such phenomena have been reported are seeking some form of material gain such as securing a new house to rent in a more desirable area. There is always the publicity factor to be borne in mind. Some people enjoy the notoriety of living in a house where strange things happen.

However, the actual state of mind of the person mainly concerned or the nature of the relationships between those living in the affected place should always be examined. Traumatic incidents such as sudden bereavements, a family member committing suicide; these may lie behind the strange events which are being observed. If the person or persons can be helped to work through the feelings associated with their traumas the poltergeist activity may well slowly cease. If those concerned are Christian believers then, in addition to counselling and sympathetic listening, a celebration of the Holy Eucharist and the blessing of the house may well prove to be the answer. If, however, there is no Christian commitment on the part of those who have sought help to get rid of this unwelcome activity this debases a Sacrament and encourages belief in some kind of magic acts. In any case it is likely that once the phenomenon has been discussed and externalised it will cease to occur.

Those who counsel the bereaved will know that, from time to time, the grieving person will see a paranormal vision of the person who has died. The most obvious explanation is that the person concerned refuses to believe that their loved one is dead and unconsciously manufactures the hallucinatory experience. Such happenings will be heard sympathetically but as progress is made in dealing with the bereavement, the appearances will cease.

Yet another source of unusual visitations has been described as the spirits of *the unquiet dead*. I was briefly involved in a case where an elderly man had died who had suffered a broken relationship with a particular religious community. Subsequent to the breakdown he had sought to denigrate that community on every possible occasion. When he died the young couple who bought his house were experiencing a variety of strange happenings including poltergeist phenomena. His troubled spirit had not found rest. In this case a celebration of the Holy Eucharist was arranged and prayers were said for his repose and the house was blessed. No further strange happenings were recorded.

Although it is difficult to discern between psychological imbalance and real spirit activity, as indicated previously, care must always be taken not to give the impression that what is happening is some kind of magical incantation. The blessing of the house and the celebration of the Sacrament will, in almost every case, be the answer.

☞ *Give thought to how you might act when faced with such phenomena. Perhaps your first course of action should be to pray for wisdom and guidance. Beware of dismissing such people as strange and weird. However odd may be the happenings they describe, they are needy people who deserve your understanding and help.*

Questions for personal written answers or to promote discussion

1. *How would you respond to the statement that belief in a personal devil and consequent demonic possession is a reversion to out-dated superstitions?*

2. *Dr John Grange wrote a letter to the Churches' Council for Health and Healing Newsletter in which he referred to a visit to Indonesia in which a distinguished Indonesian physician and scientist told him that although he did not believe in the existence of demons at the intellectual level, he found it very hard to shake off his fear of demons, especially in the dark hours of the night, because he had been raised in a culture in which the demonic was regarded as an ever-present reality. Dr Grange's comment was that it is not demons themselves but belief in demons which needs to be exorcised. How do you respond to this?*

3. *Do we tend to spend too much time thinking of personal evil dispositions and not enough time thinking and acting about social and community evil, which may require our being more active in political decision-making?*

4. *It has been suggested that a belief in demonic possession can be used as an escape from personal responsibility. Work out how you might try to discern if this is so in a particular situation which is brought to your notice.*

5. *How might you test out the nature of unusual phenomena which have been presented to you by an obviously needy person who has been troubled by strange happenings?*

Alive in the Spirit

If you are reading (or hearing) these words, then you have every reason to believe that you are alive!

Become conscious of your breathing. Listen to your pulse. Yes, your heart is beating. You are alive.

But reflect now upon your limited experience of *aliveness*. It is possible that you have discovered for yourself the thrill of sailing. You have felt the power of the wind taking hold of the sails and thrusting the yacht forward, cutting a passage through the waves. You may be alive in this particular way. Many have never experienced this thrill.

You may have become aware of the sheer power displayed by the animals whose natural home is in the jungle. You may have witnessed (from a safe hiding place) the charge of a herd of wild elephants. You may have seen a lion chasing a pack of deer and picking one out for the kill. An exciting but terrifying experience which has burnt itself into your memory. This aspect of aliveness may have become part of you whilst on safari in Africa. But many millions of people have never come to life in this way.

You may have experienced the joy of creativity by bringing a scene to life in oils or watercolours or plain black and white. It now decorates your wall or stands in a frame on your sideboard. It is often admired and though you may have painted it years ago it still brings you a thrill. The scene came to life within you and then you were able to give it life through your artistic skills. Many folk have tried to do the same but somehow that part of them which could produce a picture lies dormant. Or it may not exist at all.

So what does it mean to be alive in the Spirit? Sometimes people talk about it in extravagant ways. They tell of tremendous changes happening in a moment of time. My personal and pastoral experience is that the Spirit gives life in many ordinary ways, often bringing about small but significant changes in our lives. A Ford worker from Dagenham had become part of an Industrial Group which a young colleague of mine had started. They were doing Bible study and relating their discoveries to their lives within the car industry and within their trade union. I invited one of their number to tell us what engaging in this particular operation had achieved. His description was encapsulated in four words: 'I feel switched on.'

Another friend had begun to experiment in realising every day that he was invited to be alive in the Spirit. His description was just as graphic: 'I have been lifted out of the Church's filing system.'

So now, on the basis of the Bible's witness and the above bold declarations, let us deliberately seek to come alive in the Spirit in some new part of our lives. For instance we can legitimately seek . . .

A deeper awareness

Remember:

> the love of God has been poured out in our hearts through
> the Holy Spirit who has been given to us.   *Romans 5:5*

> For Jesus' nearness gave them heart,
> To venture, come what would.
> The love of Jesus bade them share,
> Their life, possessions, food.
> The mind of Jesus gave them speech
> That all men understood.
>
> *Ian M. Fraser*

Come, great Spirit, come.

Have you ever reflected upon the connection between the notion of being 'alive in the Spirit' and 'the grace of our Lord Jesus Christ'? What the Spirit does is to enable us to become aware of the significance of the events in the life of Jesus. As we listen to what he said and did in the years when he dwelt among us, so the Spirit brings the stories and sayings to life. To be alive in Christ and to be alive in the Spirit are two ways of describing the same experience.

> We must also trust the Holy Spirit,
> who works within us
> through the mystery of grace.
> If we let him, he forms
> a kind of instinctive judgement
> with regard to those elements
> which are compatible with Christianity
> and those that are not;
> this is exactly what we mean
> by the gifts of the Holy Spirit.
>
> *Bernard Cooke*

Come, great Spirit, come.

A second gift consequent upon our being alive in the Spirit is ...

Increased sensitivity

Those who are alive in the Spirit become more sensitive to their own needs and to the needs of others. Sometimes in a counselling relationship we get a strong feeling that we should move out towards the needy person in a specific way. This is partly the result of our training and experience, but there is, from time to time, a sensitivity which is a direct gift of the Spirit. As slowly and carefully we respond to it, so the feelings are confirmed.

> O let thy sacred will
> All thy delight in me fulfil!
> Let me not think an action mine own way,
> But as thy love shall sway,
> Resigning up the rudder to thy skill.
> *George Herbert*

Silence is often the setting in which we find our sensitivity increased. 'Study to be quiet,' suggests St Paul (1 Thessalonians 4:11 – AV). A relationship can be deepened when two people agree together to be quiet in God's presence. A fractious business meeting can be transformed when those present decide to listen to God and then really listen to each other. Sensitivity as a gift of being 'alive in the Spirit' can save us from dropping many bricks and hurting others through thoughtlessness.

> There are two ways
> of bringing into communion
> the diversity of particular gifts:
> the love of sharing
> and the sharing of love.
> Thus the particular gift becomes common
> to him who has it:
> he who has it
> communicates by sharing,
> he who has it not
> participates by communion.
> *Baldwin of Ford*

Come, great Spirit, come.

There is yet another gift shared with us as we come to life in the Holy Spirit . . .

Guidance

Some people lay remarkable claims to guidance in the daily affairs of life, even to the point of being guided to an empty car parking space. I have never been conscious of such detailed guidance but I have sometimes realised that I could have walked the distance in the time involved in looking for such a space! Perhaps this realisation was guidance in itself! Years ago I was told that if I was faced by two or even three possible courses of action then I should travel along each one in my imagination and do it prayerfully, and along one of those ways I should feel a greater sense of peace. For me this has worked on just one or two occasions when major decisions have been called for.

God also guides by giving to us moments of perception. C. S. Lewis described one such precious moment as follows:

> I was going up Headington Hill on the top of a bus. I was aware
> that I was holding something at bay; shutting something out . . .
> I chose to open, to unbuckle, to unloose the rein . . .

As a young man I sat quietly in a corner of Chester Cathedral. I was troubled in spirit about what lay immediately ahead of me. Suddenly it happened. A quiet sense of assurance with an accompanying experience of inward warmth. That moment was to me a real experience of guidance.

> Christ promised an insecure world
> to his disciples
> but gave them the security of a guide.
> This guide is the Holy Spirit.
> *Ladislas M. Orsy*

Come, great Spirit, come.

Notice how awareness, sensitivity and guidance are all closely linked. The comments and illustrations applied to them individually and separately above could have been applied significantly to all three.

> O come and dwell in me,
> Spirit of power within,
> And bring the glorious liberty
> From sorrow, fear and sin.
> *Charles Wesley*